GROWTH

GROWTH

Flipping The Script On My
Life-Changing Moment

DYLAN FINN

a memoir

This book is a memoir. It reflects the author's present recollections of experiences over time. Some names and characteristics have been changed, some events have been compressed, and some dialogue has been recreated.

Published by Growth Enterprises Sea Girt NJ

DEDICATION

I dedicate this book to the millions of people
that hit a bump in the road.
To the people that are at a point in their life
where times have gotten hard, and they don't know
whether they should turn left or turn right.
I want you to know that the
helpless and lost feeling can go away.
I want you to know that these are,
although they might not seem like it,
some of the most important moments of your life,
and can help you create your future.
This book will teach you to learn from the hard times and
grow from your suffering.
I hope this book helps you create the life you desire.

ACKNOWLEDGEMENTS

I would like to thank my mom,
for showing me what true strength is when times get hard,
and for raising me with pure love.
A very special thanks to Paul Melella,
for this book would not be possible without you.
Thank you for showing me infinite power.
And lastly, a special thank you to my 21-year-old self.
For when life gave you ten reasons to give up,
you kept pushing to discover a work ethic and faith
that made you the man you are today.

PART ONE

HOW I BECAME THE MAN
I AM TODAY

A MIRACLE

THE FACT I WAS EVEN BORN WAS A MIRACLE. Before I came along, my mom had seven miscarriages. Seven! But my mom was positive she wanted to be a mother, so she adopted a baby boy. She adopted him from a family in Florida. There was no specific reason why the family wanted to put him up for adoption; they just knew they couldn't afford a baby and parenthood just wasn't meant for them. So, my parents took him home and named the baby Shane.

About a year and a half later, my mother and my father adopted a baby girl. The birth mother was a nurse in Florida who worked the night shift and knew that she couldn't make ends meet between working and being a mother, so she went through with the pregnancy and put the baby girl up for adoption. My mom and dad decided to name the girl Kelli. My father is an Irish man and felt the name Kelli carried on the heritage. My parents didn't care whether they were biological or not; they loved their family more than anything in the world. Shane and Kelli were now their kids—two beautiful babies.

Right when everything started to come together, life

threw my parents another curveball. Shortly after putting in the papers to adopt Kelli, my mom found out she was pregnant. Because of her history, she didn't really get excited. After seven miscarriages, you just begin to expect this time to be like the last. However, my mother went on to have a full-term pregnancy, which had never happened to her before. When she asked the doctor how this could be possible, he said, "Donna, there's no medical reason. I can't give you science as to why it's possible." He looked at her and said, "Do you believe in miracles? Because this truly is a miracle child!"

Somehow, someway, I was the one that made it out. It's funny, you look at it like: what was so different about the time my mom was pregnant with me compared to the other seven times? Probably not much. The doctors at the hospital were star-struck. One of the nurses approached my mom after I was born and said, "Seven miscarriages and this one made it out, truly is amazing!" Grinning from cheek to cheek, my mom agreed with her, speechless because there was no way to explain why this one made it out. The lady looked at my mom and said, "You should name him Joseph. Joseph, in biblical terms, is the name for *Miracle Child*."

My mom already had the first name Dylan picked out for me but no middle name. My mother was a gym teacher, and she had this one student who stuck out more than the rest. This student wasn't always clowning around like the rest of the eighth grade boys and was always a leader. He made sure if he saw a girl being picked on, he would slide in and tell the boys to stop. He was smart, outgoing, and always trying to go the extra mile. As my mom tried to think of a good name for her newborn, this student was a great example of what she wanted her son to be like. This student's name was Dylan.

So, once I was born, she thought, "He truly is a blessing. Maybe miracle child is a fitting middle name!" So, I was named Dylan Joseph Finn.

SEA GIRT

WE WERE RAISED IN THE SMALL BEACH TOWN of Sea Girt, New Jersey. Sea Girt consisted of mostly upper-middle-class families and had a population of about 1,800 people. I don't know how many people live in your town, but this is very small.

We went to Sea Girt Elementary School from kindergarten through eighth grade. Sea Girt Elementary had approximately 180 kids in total, around twenty kids per grade. It varied every year, but for the most part, my grade consisted of fifteen boys and five girls. Imagine how hard it was being one of those five girls.

Sea Girt was a rather small, one-level brick school. Since it was only one floor, there were no stairs. It had a quiet road on one side and a highway on the other. We had a turf that we played football on and basketball courts where we could lower the rims. Instead of keeping the rims at ten feet and getting better at our game, we would lower the rims to seven feet and would each pick which NBA player we wanted to play as. Next thing I knew, I was Kobe Bryant shooting fadeaways and dunking with ease.

Sea Girt was pretty awesome. My house was all of a two-block walk from the beach. In between those two blocks was Crescent Park, which was the spot where people sometimes went to go smoke weed. About two more blocks south was The Army Camp, a military base where they stored tanks, jets, and other important military stuff. Being the stupid, delinquent kids we were, we would go and try to sneak around some of the stuff, which usually ended with a security guard chasing us out.

Being ten-year-old boys, this was like Heaven on earth. Growing up, kids play with tanks and army toys, but we had the real thing a block away from us! I can recall one Saturday adventure where two of my friends and I were messing around the tanks. We noticed one of them wasn't locked, so what a great idea to go inside. After being inside for about ten minutes, we heard a loud and deep voice through a speaker say, "No unauthorized attendees are allowed in any of our—" but before he even finished the sentence, we were up and running. There was an army camp security guard on a golf cart about twenty feet from the tank. We ran at full force as he tried to catch us. We hopped the fence and we were home free. What two minutes prior was pure fear, was now endless laughter!

Growing up in a close-knit community, everyone knew everyone, and probably knew your parents' names, too. When you live in a small town like Sea Girt, there's no such thing as a secret. The same kids I went to school with I went to church with, I went to little league baseball games with, and I interacted with every day, everywhere.

About smack in the middle of town there was a breakfast joint called Ray's Café. Ray's Café was the definition of a small-town café. You knew every time you walked in that the same waitress was going to be waiting tables, the same chef that has been there forever was going to be flipping pork rolls, and Ray was going to be running around every inch of the café making sure all needs were met. You knew that the same guys were going to be sitting at the counter that were sitting there yesterday, and you knew the bacon was going to be crisp and ready to be served.

The best part about Ray's Café was it brought in the youngest of young kids from Sea Girt Elementary School, while also bringing in all the dads during their lunch break. The reason being there was only one Ray's Café, where you could walk in with mud on your shorts from stickball and the waitress laughed and found you a table. A place where your pork roll and chocolate milk was $7, but since you only had $5, Ray told you to just pay next time. Oh yeah, that meant to pay in cash—there was no taking cards. And the truth is, everyone had a smile on their face.

If you lived in Sea Girt, you went to Ray's Café. And not only did you go to Ray's Café, but you also probably went there every weekend. It wasn't just where you went to get breakfast. It was where you went for food, laughs, and a good social community.

THE FINN KIDS

MY BROTHER GREW UP TO BE A SURFER AND skateboarder, and his biggest worry in the world is if the surf is going to be good today. Shane rolls with the flow, finding the positive in every negative situation. He really is one of the happiest dudes you'd ever meet.

My older sister, Kelli, could be placed in a room of Harvard graduates—even at the age of fifteen—and was most likely the smartest in the room. Kelli is a gift. Kelli enjoyed reading, movies, plays, and so much stuff that the average teenager didn't really enjoy. She was more mature than the crowd. She ended up getting a full-ride scholarship to Fordham University and fulfilling her purpose.

Then there was me. The athlete of the family. I played basketball and baseball my whole life, and for the most part it came rather easily to me. I was always a people person. I loved hanging out with my friends and socializing. I was nothing like Kelli, but school came easily to me.

For being radically different from each other, we all got along pretty well. We all had our differences, but we respected that about each other. If there was one thing our parents taught us growing up, it was respect. It was knowing that I thought baseball was the coolest sport in the world and everyone should like it, but my sister didn't. She thought it was cool to be the smartest in the room and get scholarships from Ivy League schools. Now, looking back, I agree with her and think that is cool, but our parents taught us to accept that everyone is different whether you agree with them or not. That's life. No two people are the same.

MR. AND MRS. FINN

MY FATHER—THIS MAN IS THE MOST LOVED guy in the room. Dan Finn has a positivity that is unmatchable. I would come back from a little league game after having three strikeouts and I would throw my baseball bag in the garage. "God damn I f-ing suck!" He would look at me and go, "D, calm down. You might've struck out three times, but when you were foul tipping the ball your swing looked amazing!" In anger, I would look at him and say, "Dad, stop, it was just a foul tip. I think I should quit," and he would put his arm around me and say, "Keep your head up, D. Let's go to the batting cages tomorrow. The only way to get better is to practice."

So, I did. I loved baseball. And then when I had a good game—two singles and a double—my dad was the first person in the crowd to be cheering. And then when the game was over, my dad and I went to Hoffman's so he could treat me to some ice cream. Lots of love.

Now for my mom—well, I saved her for last in the family for a reason.

This lady did it all for us. What separated my mom

from the rest was the values she instilled in us. When your waiter brings over your order, you ALWAYS say thank you. Even if it took longer than you would like. If you and a girl are both walking in a door, you ALWAYS hold the door for her first. It isn't that it is a nice thing to do, it's that it is the *right thing to do*. If we had to be at a basketball game by 7, my mom made sure we would be there at 6:55. She taught me if you're not five minutes early, you're late. If we wanted to go to a friend's house, she would drive us there no matter what she had going on. She had us where we had to be, when we had to be there, and not a minute late.

Growing up and being able to look back now, the best way to describe it is unconditional love. That's what makes my mom special to me. Through the high highs and through the low lows, through the times when we were really just being pain-in-the-ass children, love found a way to always be the front page of our story. And that story has really good memories—it also has really hard times. But like I said, love always found a way to be highlighted on each page.

And we also made lots of time for the fun stuff. We were always skiing, at the skatepark, at the beach—wherever we wanted to be, we were there. She was a mom who made sure her kids were always happy. That was her biggest priority. Making sure we were happy before she was happy. Sad, but true. That's how much she loves us. She prioritized us more than herself.

I had a lot of amazing people in my life that influenced me to work harder and be a good person. I had a mom who raised us to be so driven that I would come from school so excited to show her that I got an eighty-five percent on my science test, and she would look at it, nod her head, and tell me I'm capable of a ninety percent. I know what you're thinking: that's harsh. No, I loved that. That taught me to always go one step further.

As my mom's father, my grandpa used to say to us, "Good, better, best, never let it rest 'til your good is better and your better is best." To this day, I still apply this quote. I apply this quote because you might be happy with being average, but you know you're capable of more. Shoot for the stars. Don't stop at average. Get to average and work up even higher. You are capable of so much more than you think you are.

My parents were very big skiers. So, naturally, we were born to be skiers. I clearly don't remember this, but my mom tells stories of when I was two years old, she would put me on skis, and I would ride down the mountain in between her legs. It sounds risky, doesn't it? But my mom knew she was good and wanted to raise us to be good skiers so we could enjoy our family winters in Pennsylvania.

As we got older, I stuck with skiing, always doing terrain park, trying to be a showoff by doing 360s and rails. The terrain park consisted of rails, jumps, and obstacles making skiing harder than it needed to be. Kelli was a skier, but she took it rather carefully. She was happy just enjoying the moment, playing some music, and taking in the scenery.

Now for Shane—Shane was a snowboarder, but he was similar to me. He liked doing tricks and taking risks that he probably shouldn't have been doing. We for sure had some good times. We were like each other's worst influence, talking one another into taking chances that we both knew we weren't good enough to be doing.

Now here's the best part about our ski trips. My parents would rent a house in Shawnee, Pennsylvania for the winter, January through March. We would go skiing every weekend. Sea Girt Elementary would have ninth period be a club every Friday. Each student got to pick which club interested them the most. Some people picked gym, some people picked cooking, some picked art. There was no wrong answer.

Yet when ninth block would come around every Friday, my mom would sign us out of school and we would hit the road. We would get an hour's head start driving to Pennsylvania. It was awesome! Every Friday, around the seventh or eighth block, I would start to get the itch. "C'mon Dylan, only twenty-five more minutes till we're skiing," I would tell myself. "C'mon Dylan, we're almost there." And, naturally, this made it take even longer. But every winter, every Friday, we were beyond excited to go to Shawnee and get in a weekend of skiing.

I'm grateful for my childhood. I have a lot of unforgettable memories. And during the hard times, a lot of life lessons were learned. Looking back, I seriously wouldn't change a thing. From the people in my life, to where I was, to the mistakes I made, all of them were worth it.

After middle school, I headed off to Manasquan High School.

TEENAGE YEARS

MANASQUAN HIGH SCHOOL WAS A DECENTLY sized high school, which was not too big, not too small. At Manasquan, you were either an athlete, a partier, a stoner, or a brainiac. I was a mixture of an athlete and a partier. My parents were always cool with me drinking as long as it was in moderation. Well, I didn't always do that. But I learned lessons and grew from them. I had a great friend group. We had our fair share of fun and did stupid stuff.

I was a pretty good athlete in high school. I played basketball and I played baseball. My sophomore year, I played JV basketball and varsity baseball. Since I was playing up for my age, I was hanging out with older guys. In doing so, I was drinking and partying more than I should have been.

For instance, one night, I went to a party where I drank more than I should have. When I got home, it led to me running my mouth more than I should have, getting me in some trouble. My mom, being the cool mother she was, told me to go to my room and go to bed. After getting to my room, I saw my buddy had texted me to see if I wanted to come over for some deck beers. Being the overconfident teenager I was, I thought this was a great idea. So, I snuck out. After about twenty minutes of being out, I hadn't gotten any text from mom or dad. "Let's go! I'm in the clear. I should do this more often. This is great!" I went to my friend's house, hung out, had a great time, and biked home around 4 am. Just to get home to realize I was locked out of the house. "Okay, stay calm," I told myself. "Go to sleep on the back couch, wake up at 7 am, and when dad unlocks the backdoor to let Bandit out, sneak into your room." What sounded like such a great idea in my head never happened that way. I woke up to my dad standing over me asking,

"What are you doing?"

But I was always friendly, and I was always nice. Whether it was my friends, a coach, or a teacher, I always found a way to be on their good side. This helped me a lot in high school. I flew by rather easily. I wasn't a genius, but I knew how to get good grades.

Not only did I make good friends at Manasquan, I also formed some relationships with coaches that I'll have for the rest of my life. My basketball coach, Andrew Bilodeau, still reaches out to me today. For my baseball coaches, Mr. Waldyer and B Lee are two guys I can reach out to whenever I need them. Playing sports and seeing these guys every day for four years straight forged a bond that made them treat us like we were basically their kids.

I dated a girl for three years at Manasquan. Looking back, we made some really great memories. Although it didn't work out, I know that was for the better. I learned so much from that relationship and grew so much as a person.

Manasquan High School gave me some great memories and some friendships that will last a lifetime. I wouldn't change a thing about where I was or who I was. I loved Manasquan and the people that came with it.

As I started to look for colleges, I was lost. I didn't know whether I wanted a football school or a beach school. I didn't know if I wanted to be in the Northeast or if I wanted to be in the South. I applied to seven different schools. And they were all over the map: Florida State, University of Georgia, University of South Carolina, College of Charleston, University of Delaware, James Madison University, and Rutgers.

After doing some visits and checking schools out, there was one that felt right for me. One that I visited and knew this was where I belonged: College of Charleston. After my first visit to Charleston, it just felt so right; it was such a beautiful city, and it was only a few miles away from the beach. Coming from my small beach town, it was the closest thing to it. And wow, I loved the way it felt. It felt like home away from home.

MAKING IT DOWN SOUTH

CHARLESTON WAS BEYOND WHAT A NINE-teen-year-old college student could dream of. More than I ever could ask for. From the people, to the bars/restaurants, to the activities, boredom didn't exist. I was very fortunate, right from the start I met an awesome group of dudes.

My suitemate, Mobes—we formed a brotherhood right off the bat. Down the hall in my dorm, Colin—we connected right away. Making your way up to the fourth floor was where you could find Jerry. Well, not always. He had a tendency to get a little lost some nights. But making friends and living in the same building as them, that was a pretty fun lifestyle to live. I partied, went to the beach, played intramural sports, and went on road trips. It was all too good to be true. We went to a college in a city that consisted of bars, and at some of those bars you could show a piece of cardboard as ID and they'd let you in. I was going to class Monday through Thursday and then living off the walls from Thursday night on. It was fun. But looking back, that social life was mixed with a good amount of unhealthy. Instead of going to Charleston to come back with a good education, I started prioritizing fun before anything.

My freshman year of college, my dad had a stroke. It was scary. It took me back a step. I remember I couldn't comprehend the fact it was actually real until I saw him lying in a hospital bed. Being twenty years old and seeing your dad lie in a hospital bed, well, that will wake you up real fast. My family didn't know what the outcome would be. I flew home from Charleston to check on him, and, more so, to check on my mother to make sure she was mentally okay. My father changed from his stroke. He was speaking with a slur. He was forgetting important people in our lives along with names, and he couldn't quite interact with people the same way he used to. But if there was one thing that stayed the same, it was this man's positivity. He nearly died, but he was still smiling cheek-to-cheek and laughing his ass off.

I remember the first time I walked into his hospital room. Every emotion possible was running through my body. I was so excited to see him after nearly losing him, yet also terrified because I didn't know what I was walking in on. I remember every step I took felt like I had 100-pound weights on my feet. It was so hard to walk in that room. The dad I had known would be smiling cheek-to-cheek saying, "Yee-haw," but I knew this was not what I was walking into.

What I found when I finally saw him was that he was emotionless. He still looked the same. He was sitting up with a smile on his face, but he couldn't carry on a conversation the way he used to. All we could do was support him, so that is what we did, and he has recovered so much since that day.

WAKEUP CALL

FRESHMAN YEAR WAS A WAKEUP CALL FOR ME. I went from living in a house with lots of love to being on my own. I was lucky, I had a really cool roommate and two suitemates I knew from home. My roommate was from South Carolina. We bonded over the fact we both loved sports. We hung out with different crowds, but always got along in our room.

It was tough. I went from living in a middle-class home with people that were all similar to me to starting from step one: meeting new people, some that I liked, some that I didn't, and trying to adjust to a new lifestyle.

In high school I had an awesome group of friends and an amazing girlfriend. Life was good. Now it was like none of that existed anymore. It all went out the window. No one gave a fuck about the past. The way I like to look at it, now that times have changed, is that it was a wake-up call. It was a sign that life wasn't always easy. Life gets hard, and you have two choices: cry about it and give up or learn from it and grow. I think you can figure out which was the right choice for me to make.

I learned from it. A lot. And looking back, I really do think I grew for the better. I made some lifelong friends and I also learned what it was like to live outside of our small bubble of a hometown. I learned that life changes. People, places, locations... it will always be changing. It changed me to learn how to adapt to new circumstances and not give up.

I really enjoyed being in Charleston. I had an awesome group of friends. I began my time at Charleston as a Finance major, but after my freshman year I had a conversation with an upperclassman. He said to me, "You have such a social personality and you're outgoing. You should think about doing Hospitality and Tourism as your major. You could do something along the lines of event planning, wedding planning, etc. This way you're literally just socializing for a living."

And, well, I certainly loved the sound of that. So, at that point I changed my major and I declared a Hospitality and Tourism major. I always had a social, outgoing personality, plus I was in a city that consisted of bars and hotels, so I felt like Hospitality and Tourism was a fitting major for me.

I enjoyed the classes I had to take for my major. They consisted of learning about hotels, bars, weddings, and more. A lot of the classes I had to take focused on socializing and working on building relationships with other people. Hospitality was being able to handle the people around you and, well, that came rather easily to me. I always found a way to get along with the crowd that happened to be handed to me. Whether it was three guys or two girls, athletes or academics, I found a way to make it work. It was a good switch from crunching numbers in finance. For God's sake, we even had a Hospitality and Tourism class on beer and wine tasting. It was a college kid's dream class.

I definitely started to spiral out of control a little bit, though. The lifestyle I was living in Charleston consisted of drinking three to four nights a week and making decisions I shouldn't be making. Whether it was acting so obnoxious that I got kicked out of bars, or as simple as skipping class to stay in my dorm to play Xbox and go to the beach, I was consistently finding myself doing what I shouldn't have been doing.

Then COVID-19 happened. It was March of 2020, my sophomore spring semester. We were all sent home and the world was put on lockdown. Going from a college lifestyle to not being able to leave your parents' home wasn't exactly fun. Most people don't experience a nationwide pandemic smack in the middle of their college lifestyle. We went from sharing mixed drinks and not giving a single care in the world to all of a sudden not being able to stand within six feet of someone. You couldn't walk out your front door without a mask. For God's sake, some people were wearing two masks. It was madness. It was like a parallel universe we were living in.

However, my friends and I already signed our lease in Charleston for the next year before COVID-19 hit. So, we all went back down to Charleston at the end of July. Charleston was doing online classes, so we were still in school without actually going to the school and attending in-person classes. Back in New Jersey, the COVID rules were out the wazoo. In Charleston, at first, it was almost like some people made the choice to believe it wasn't real. Yeah, we were in online classes, but there were some bars and restaurants that were fully functioning. It was when it really got blown up on the news that places began to have greater restrictions. It was a crazy time for everyone. Depression was at an all-time high, and people were scared to leave their houses. It was an unfamiliar world, and this radical change created a void in events for college students.

Finally, after a long time of living like this, we got amazing news. One of our favorite bands, Mt. Joy, was playing live in Asheville, North Carolina. It may sound so generic to you now, but, in 2020, live music was unheard of. The fact that we could go to a concert was the best news we had heard in a year. It was a worldwide pandemic—concerts just didn't exist.

With this being said, there were some rules and regulations to be followed. It was a concert, but people had to stay in their parked cars. Or, if not in parked cars, within a ten-foot radius. Also, everyone had to have a mask. Anyway, we packed our bags and made our way to North Carolina. I'm not sure if you have ever been to Asheville, but this place is like Disney for twenty-one year olds. A lot of bars, mountains, and, most importantly, refreshing air. A few miles from our Airbnb, there was a hiking trail that went through these nice mountains. As we kept hiking, we came across a waterfall. The carefree, young, and spontaneous college kids we were, we all took our shirts off and jumped in the waterfall. I felt like I was in Heaven.

Well, until I almost was in Heaven…

SKATEBOARDS AND HIKES

I WENT TO ASHEVILLE ON OCTOBER 2, 2020 with a bunch of friends. It was a Friday. Being college kids, we had our stupid fun. I was drinking, doing drugs, the whole nine yards. It was the first time we were able to have freedom since before COVID. We had an Airbnb that consisted of around thirty to thirty-five college kids. Some were sleeping in beds, some were sleeping on couches, and some were even sleeping on the floor. It was a free-for-all.

I woke up on October 3—and now just hearing that date makes my whole body shake, it scares me just thinking about it. I woke up on October 3 to my friend pouring shots of tequila. It was eight in the morning and the madness had already begun!

I walked outside. God, the air was so fresh it was the healthiest I had felt since before COVID. It didn't seem like a pandemic existed here. The air was way too pure for there to be a deadly virus going around. All was good in the world. Well, at least I thought.

I walked outside. I had some friends just hanging on

the porch, and I had one friend skateboarding down the road out front. It wasn't just any road; it was pretty steep.

My friend was bombing this hill. But he was doing it with ease. He was a pretty good skateboarder, and he was making it look like a breeze. So, me being the overconfident invincible guy I thought I was, I had asked him if I could hop on the skateboard. He passed the board over to me and goes, "Go for it Dfinn, bomb the hill."

I grabbed the skateboard, went about halfway up the hill, and got ready to go down. I didn't go to the top for a reason, because I knew I was no Tony Hawk. I was about to step foot on the board when I heard my friend call out, "DFINN! ARE YOU A PUSSY? START FROM THE TOP OF THE HILL!"

The way I have been my whole life is that I don't let anyone call me weak or a "pussy," so I got off the board and walked to the top of the hill. That was where my life changed forever. I remember everything from that day... until this moment right here:

I got to the top of the hill and I got on the board. Knowing damn well I wasn't good enough at skateboarding to skate down this hill. But the alcohol and the arrogance I had convinced me I was. So, I did it.

As I was skating, my legs started to wobble. I can still feel that moment. My legs started to wobble, and I fell. Hard. I fell and the right side of my head hit the pavement, and then the back of my head hit the pavement. Lights out. Goodnight. Dylan was no longer present.

My friends came over and helped me. I'm grateful for that. My friends said that I was extremely dazed and confused. I was out of it. I laid down and it took me a while to get up, but, finally, I did.

I have been told from a friend's perspective that, as I was going down the hill, they saw my legs start to wobble. They told me they could see my legs wobbling, and my arms started to flail. Next, my head absolutely SLAMMED the pavement. They told me it was no graceful fall. The second I hit the ground, they knew it wasn't pretty.

I don't remember this, but I called my mom. She's my best friend. I told her that I fell while skateboarding and I was really shaken up. "Did you hit your head?" asked my mom.

"Yes," I replied. "I'm okay, though." This was a red flag to her. She knew I was drinking, and drinking with head injuries isn't the best combination. She told me to go to the hospital. I told her I was okay and, of course, I didn't listen. She told me to call her back in two hours and update her on how I felt. She also told my girlfriend at the time to keep an eye on me and make sure everything was okay. So, my day went on.

I went back outside and met up with my friends. I was drinking, smoking, and doing stupid stuff college kids shouldn't be doing. As the day went on, it was time for us to go to our concert.

Since it was during the heart of COVID-19, it wasn't like any ordinary concert. There were no crowds allowed, or really being that close to each other. It was a drive-in concert. You had to stay in or near your car. Now, looking back, my friends have told me I was really out of it. A couple friends said I was slurring and making obnoxious remarks. So obnoxious that they knew, even when I'm that drunk, I wouldn't be saying stuff like that. At the time they thought it was just because I was under the influence of alcohol, but now that we know what we know, they wish they had said something sooner.

My friends lost me. Or should I say I lost them. They didn't know where I went. They knew I was fucked up, and the fact they couldn't find me was scary to them. Finally, my friend Mobes and his girlfriend found me lying down in his car trying to fall asleep. The concert wrapped up, and we all went back to the Airbnb.

———

Being the carefree college kids we were, my friends and I went out for a hike. It was two in the morning. Who goes on a hike at two in the morning? Asheville was a very beautiful place, so I understand why we wanted to, but know now it was not the right time to do so. So, we're out exploring Asheville when we come across a big statue of Jesus. Ironic.

We all stood there staring at the Jesus statue mesmerized…

At this point, somehow, I disappeared from the crowd and ventured off on my own. I love hearing the following story from my good friend's point of view:

When we got to the statue, one of my friends said he separated himself from the crowd. He looked at the statue of Jesus, and he said a prayer. He said, "Lord, I would like to say a prayer that everyone stays safe tonight. Everyone stays healthy tonight. I know we have been doing a lot of substances that could affect our health. Please, protect everyone."

While this was going on, I was still on my own somewhere exploring through Asheville.

This is the story as best I can piece together from what I have been told from friends:

At this moment, I believe four of my friends found me lying down on the pavement in the street with blood coming out of my ears, nose, and mouth. "Get down here fast, guys! Dylan's face-down, surrounded by a pool of blood, things are not okay!" yelled my friend Stef as she approached me lying on the ground.

Stef yelled to our friend Marc to go get help as she began to call 911. Although we were in the middle of the mountains and struggled getting phone service all weekend, somehow Stef's call went through. My friends rolled me over to discover my face was completely bashed in.

By this point, all of my friends could tell something bad was going on and a stampede of kids came running over to help. The lake cops got there first but it took them a good twenty to thirty minutes. Ambulance arrived around forty-five minutes to an hour after that.

My two good friends Kurtis and Kyle held me up before the ambulance arrived. Fortunately, my friend Kurtis was a lifeguard, and he was able to apply some of his CPR training on me. Kyle took his shirt off to apply pressure to the bleeding on my head.

I was told that, all of a sudden, fear filled the air. I was told my heart was still beating, but my eyes wouldn't open and I wasn't moving. The party was over now. The shit that was so fun wasn't so fun anymore. Shit got serious. People weren't in the carefree "life is good" mood anymore.

While I was taken in the ambulance, I was told, everyone that was singing and dancing around before were now huddled around the living room, eyes closed, arms around each other, praying. Praying that things would turn out the slightest bit okay.

PART 2
9-1-1

PURE FAITH

MY GIRLFRIEND AT THE TIME CALLED MY MOM crying and said, "Mrs. Finn, something terrible has happened," as her voice was trembling. "Dylan collapsed, we're not sure how, but we think he's breathing. He's making a gurgling sound, and he has blood coming out of his ears, nose, and mouth. We called 911 and they're on the way." That's one way to wake up a mother.

When paramedics came, I was intubated immediately. Anyhow, the ambulance got me to Mission Hospital in Asheville, North Carolina.

Mission Hospital called my mom. I'm no parent, but I could imagine that receiving a call at 3 in the morning from a hospital in North Carolina about your son isn't exactly ideal. They said to her, "We just need your permission to do whatever we can to keep Dylan alive. He is in very serious condition, and we need your approval to do whatever it takes." My mom said, "Please do what you need," and started packing for a flight to Asheville, North Carolina.

Now, emotions were heightened in Asheville, and emotions were heightened in New Jersey. No matter where it happens, no parent wants to get a call about their son being seriously injured. But it certainly didn't help my mom's feelings knowing she had an hour drive to the airport and a three-hour plane ride to digest all of this.

While my mom started to pack her bags getting ready to make a trip, she got another call from the hospital. This time it was the hospital chaplain. "Donna, when you arrive at Mission Hospital, we will have spiritual guidance awaiting you," the chaplain explained. "We are already helping some of Dylan's friends that brought him to the hospital, and we recommend you get some as well," she continued telling my mom. The reason hospitals do this is because they wanted my mom to know that the situation was very grave. She told my mom she was praying for me, and she would be there when my mom got to the hospital.

Looking back, we now know the reason the chaplain made this call was to prepare my mom for the very worst.

By the time my mom got to Asheville, I was in a non-induced medical coma. If you don't know what a non-induced coma is, it means they didn't put me in a coma—I just stopped breathing. I needed to be intubated, which had already happened when the ambulance picked me up. I had tubes going into my nose, supplying me with oxygen. I was in a hospital bed that was caged in so I couldn't fall out. I also had a feeding tube right above my belly button since I was unable to feed myself.

The doctors gave me a CT scan, and the scan showed four fractures to the skull and four brain hemorrhages. As a

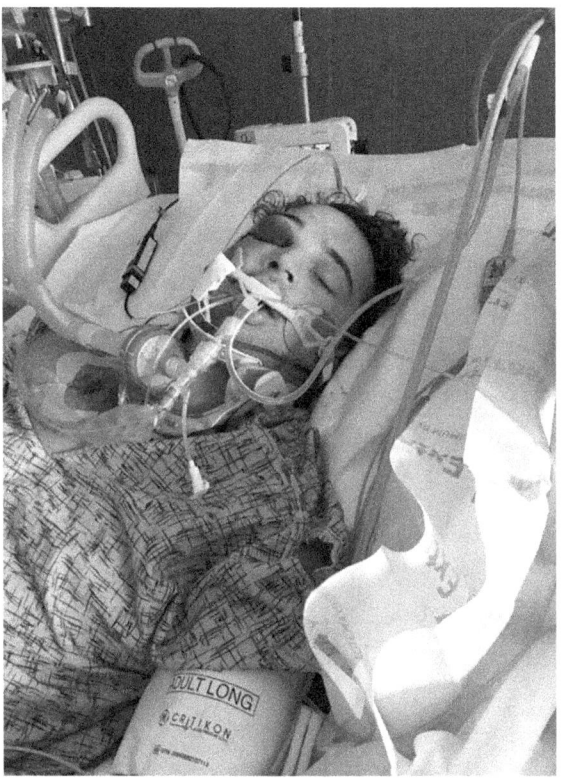

result, the doctors did a craniectomy to relieve the pressure in my brain and put a camera in the top of my head that would record the pressure in my brain. The pressure was so high from the four fractures to my skull that it needed to be monitored in the event they would have to do a craniectomy on the other side of my head.

When the team of doctors met with my mom, they explained to her that I was going to be in a neuro ICU (Intensive Care Unit) because I had four fractures to my skull. I had a fracture in my right temporal lobe, my basilar, my left temporal lobe, and my frontal lobe. On top of that, I also fractured my T6 and T7 vertebrae in my back. "Due to the severity of Dylan's injury, he is going to have 24/7 around-the-clock care. Not every patient gets this. Dylan is just on such high alert, we need eyes on him every second," the doctors told my mom.

Yikes! Not exactly what a mother wants to hear.

The doctor went on to say, "We're not here to give you false hope, Mrs. Finn. We're not going to make it sound like Dylan is better than he really is. I've seen people with much less serious traumatic brain injuries, and they don't make it. I've seen people with one brain hemorrhage pass away. Dylan has four. Things aren't looking too bright. I'm sorry to tell you this, but Dylan has a ninety percent chance of passing away. You may want to fly your family out to say goodbye. We will do whatever we can to keep your son alive." Like I said before, not exactly what a mother wants to hear about their youngest child.

So, my mom got herself a hotel room in Asheville, North Carolina. My roommate, Mobes, was calling my mom multiple times a day waiting to hear good news. He wasn't getting much. My mom told him to tell our friend group to try and keep it on the down-low. *Let's not have this story spreading around until we know more. There is still so much unknown, we don't want to rush to tell anyone anything.* But naturally, the story started to spread.

When my injury happened, the hospital gave my mom back the clothes I was wearing that night. As if seeing her son's shirt covered in blood is something she would want.

Anyway, she tried to find the positive in the negative. When my mother was going to bed in her hotel room, all alone, every thought imaginable was running through her mind.

She said to herself, "My son is NOT going to die." So, she put my sneakers from the night of my injury on the pillow next to her. As scared as my mom was, she would go to bed with faith that I was going to wear those shoes home from the hospital. When she would wake up in the morning, not knowing what the day ahead could have in store, she would kiss the sneakers. When she went to bed at night, she kissed my sneakers. *Pure Faith.*

The sneakers I wore when my injury happened.

She had faith that, with a little bit of hope, a little bit of positivity, and a little bit of love, things might turn the corner for the better.

Oh yeah, and the doctor who told my mom to fly our family out to say goodbye? She ignored him. In my mom's head, if she flew our family out, that was accepting defeat. That was giving up, believing the odds of recovering from an injury this catastrophic were slim. My mom didn't want to lean towards the side of me passing away. She wanted to hold on so tightly to the side of me recovering—no matter how slim it was.

Now, by this point, my whole family knew about my injury. My siblings had two radically different viewpoints on the situation, and I love both of them for the way their minds interpreted everything.

My sister, being the intelligent girl she is, was scared shitless. She could do all the science in her head. Kelli, better than anyone, knew there was dismal hope for everything to turn out okay. To this day, this story I'm about to share still bothers me. My sister's twenty-second birthday was shortly after my accident, on October 17. Kelli didn't tell her friends about my accident. She bottled it all up and swallowed it. On her birthday, I was still in a coma with the outcome not looking too pretty.

Trying to ignore the situation and enjoy her day, Kelli and her friends were having some drinks, playing some games, when she broke out crying. "How could I be happy on my birthday when my little brother is lying in a coma?" Her friends, having no idea what she was talking about, tried comforting her. It took me a while to forgive myself for making what should have been a special day for my sister a hard one.

Shortly after, my sister took some time off from school and flew out to Asheville. Not only to check on me, but more so to check on my mom. To make sure that through all the hard times, she was in a healthy mental state.

Now for Shane. Like I said, he had a radically different outlook on the situation. My mom was calling my siblings every day just updating them on how their younger brother was doing. How things were going when she got to the hospital and what the new consensus was. And, usually, the updates weren't too good.

From what I've heard from my mom, Shane would say to her every day, "Mom, I've seen this kid go through hard times. I've seen him play baseball and basketball his whole life. Every time he got knocked down he stood up stronger than he was before. He is going to be okay. Everything will be fine."

Now, as you can imagine, my mom was listening to what the doctors who had medical degrees were saying before she was listening to what her carefree son was saying. She would say, "Shane, this isn't a high school basketball court. His brain is bleeding in four different places, and the doctors are saying he might die!" But, like I said, I love Kelli for having the knowledge to be concerned and I love Shane for having an optimistic outlook.

Each day that passed without me waking up was a bad day. There was only so much hope given. And it's known that non-induced coma patients usually don't survive more than two or three weeks. Day fourteen of being in a coma passed, with still no signs of life. As you can imagine, an extremely emotional fourteen days for my family, and more so for my mom as she was watching a child she had birthed lie in a coma.

RISE AND SHINE

DAY FIFTEEN CAME AROUND. I AWOKE.
Extremely dazed and confused, and just out of it. At first, it instantly brought joy to my mom. It didn't seem real! After about thirty minutes, once it finally settled in, what was once joy now became fear. Because now that I was awake, who was I going to be? Not the same kid who was playing baseball and basketball and partying on the weekends with his friends. No shot. I couldn't speak yet. For Christ's sake, I didn't even move yet! All I seemed to be was a corpse lying in a bed with a beating heart. The doctors approached my mom, still being extremely straightforward with her. No false hope was given whatsoever.

Even though I was awake, I couldn't speak, walk, or really move at all. The doctor pulled my mom aside. "It could take six months to a year, if ever, that Dylan can speak again. It will take six months to a year, if ever, that Dylan can walk again. He's alive, but he's not capable of much. We only know so much about the human brain, so there are no promises about what happens next." The doctors said that I might need personal help for the rest of my life. For my mom, that meant, 'What happens when I can no longer take care of Dylan?' So, she had a conversation with Kelli to let her know she might have to be my caretaker at some point in her life. Once again, one very consistent thing throughout this experience: news my mom did not want to hear.

By the way, without giving away too much, I was walking and talking within two months. I don't remember this time period very well, but, apparently, I acquired a nickname while I was living at Mission Hospital. Since my survival rate was so low, but I somehow made it out of the coma, the doctors and nurses at Mission Hospital were calling me Miracle Man. They couldn't quite figure out how I survived a catastrophic injury that was so severe. This was the same person that, somehow, his mom birthed after seven miscarriages. So, from that point on, my nickname was Miracle Man.

So, by this point, Mission Hospital did their job. Their job was to make sure I survived and to give me some therapy. And they did a damn good job of making sure this happened. To this day, I am very grateful for Mission Hospital.

Now it was time for me to go back home. But here's the problem with brain injuries. There is still so much information that we don't know about the brain, so the doctors and therapists didn't fully know how to handle my diagnosis, or what the outcome of my recovery could really be.

The doctors figured it probably wasn't the healthiest idea to put "a brain with four brain hemorrhages" on a plane at a high altitude. So, they recommended that my family get a private jet and fly me at an extremely low altitude to Kessler in West Orange, New Jersey. It is one of the best hospitals for traumatic brain injuries. They are known for their advanced brain injury programs and services. Also, it was closer to home.

A few weeks earlier one of my roommates, Mobes, started a GoFundMe page. The fund blew up with thousands of donations of all amounts. Some very large and some very small, but each and every one was heartfelt. There were donations from friends, friends of friends, family, teachers, etc. The GoFundMe was essential and helpful with my medical needs.

Just talking about this makes me tear up. Because the amount of love and support I received from this GoFundMe page saved my life. My parents didn't think it was possible, but with the love and guidance from my hometown and my college community, we fulfilled this goal. I wouldn't be who I am today if it wasn't for the support I received from this. It saved my life.

I made it to Newark, New Jersey with my mom on the jet with me. Prior to my injury, I had a very bad nicotine addiction. The nurses and my mom said that during the whole three-hour flight I was putting my hands to my lips pretending I was hitting a vape of some sort. Crazy that even though I was so out of it and barely even knew my own name, my brain still knew how to hit a vape.

Addiction really can be scary.

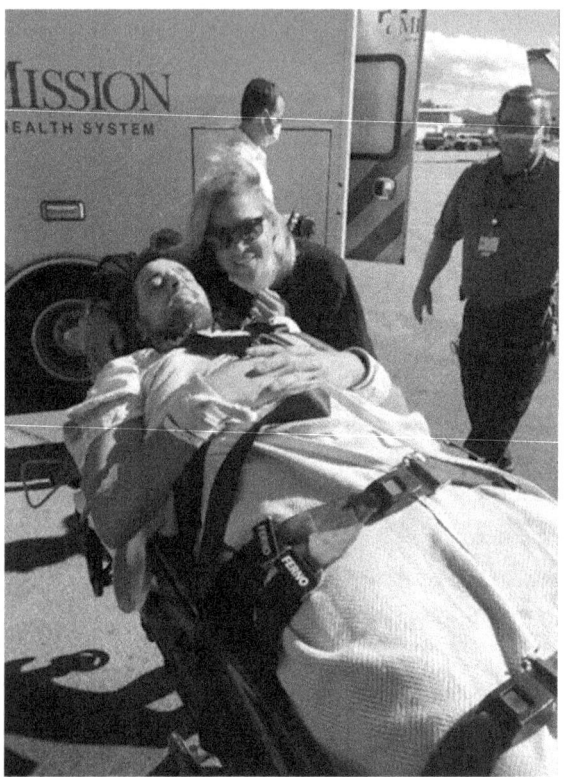

My mom and I boarding the jet

The jet that took me to Newark, New Jersey

DAY BY DAY

THE DOCTORS AT KESSLER WERE SAYING THAT it was one of the worst traumatic brain injuries they had ever seen and it was a miracle that I survived. The therapy Kessler was doing with me was essentially what parents teach their three-year-old children. They were trying to walk with me, teaching me how to spell, and doing third grade math with me. This stuff was hard for me. And, just a reminder, I had just turned twenty-one years old.

So, I started doing therapy at Kessler hospital. I don't know if it is because of pictures I have seen or just that mental images are starting to come back, but I can vaguely remember doing therapy at Kessler. I remember the physical therapy room. My therapist was holding my arm while walking me down an aisle that had walk bars for me to hold onto as they had to teach me how to walk again. And the best one I vaguely remember is playing bingo in the cafeteria and I was the only person under the age of sixty-five.

And no, I didn't win bingo.

I was really struggling to remember where I was and, even more, I was struggling to remember *who* I was. Directly across from my bed there was a banner hanging on the wall. The banner said, "Hi, my name is Dylan," hoping that I would wake up, read the banner, and it would start to come back to me who I was.

My improvement was happening very slowly, and the hope was dismal. But this part is where it really gets interesting.

I was starting to turn the corner a little bit. Doing better than I was. I have absolutely zero memory from Mission Hospital, but my memory from the first week in Kessler is where it starts to come back. The first week is still very spotty, but that was when I started to become more conscious.

I woke up one day and I felt so lonely and confused. My first idea was that I wanted to call my whole family. So, I started doing so. First, I called my mom. Then I called my Dad, then my sister, and then I called Shane. It wasn't like I was capable of making these calls on my own—I had to ask my aid to find these numbers and dial the phone for me.

It consisted of conversations that kindergarteners have. I had no idea where I was or what was going on, so the conversations were short and to the point. As I'm on the phone with Shane, I told him, "I can't remember Uncle Phil's phone number. I'm trying to call everyone in the family today since I have nothing to do here. Can you read off Phil's number to me?"

Shane went silent. Looking back, I can tell that it was a silence of fear that I didn't know what had happened to Phil.

Phil was my uncle whom we all loved. But about three

years before my injury, Phil passed away. Phil was my mom's brother. He battled alcoholism his whole life and battled some demons. "D, Phil's dead," Shane said. "Oh, right, I'm sorry, I forgot," I replied to Shane.

These were very emotional phone calls for me to make. Since my frontal lobe had a brain hemorrhage, and your frontal lobe controls your emotions, my emotions were all over the place. And after Shane and I hung up, I remember sitting back on the verge of tears. "How do I not know my uncle that I loved so dearly is dead?" I asked myself.

Now backtracking, about a few days before I made it out of the coma, when the hope for me surviving was still very low, my mom went to a psychic. My mom was asking the psychic questions about me surviving and what the outcome could possibly be. The psychic said, "Dylan will survive. Dylan made it to the gates of Heaven and saw a man he hasn't seen in a very long time. A man named Phil. Dylan reached over the gates and gave the man a hug. Being so ecstatic to see Phil, Dylan tried to hop over the gates and enter Heaven. But Phil pushed him. Phil said, 'No, Dylan, it is not your time yet.' And then he pushed him out of Heaven."

Now, prior to my injury, I was never a very spiritual person. But this story changed me. I'll explain why.

First of all, this psychic had no idea I had an uncle named Phil. But she said that I was at the gates of Heaven and a man named Phil pushed me back down. On top of that, I didn't know this story when I was in Kessler hospital. Yet the day I was calling my family, I asked Shane for Phil's phone number. I thought he was still alive. Most likely because I talked to him very recently. It all seems to align too well for it to not be true. Crazy shit.

———————

Anyhow, I was making progress. It was a process, but I was slowly moving in the right direction. My good buddy from high school, Matt, came to visit me at Kessler. He loves to tell this story, because it just shows how out of it I was. It was the first time he had seen me since I nearly died, so he walked into the room full of energy and excited to see me. He walks in and goes, "DFINN!! MY MAN, GOOD TO SEE YA! HOW YA DOIN?" I looked at him and went, "Can you help me up? I need to go to the bathroom." Here was one of my best friends in the world, and yet I looked at him and the first thing I said is help me to the bathroom?

My time at Kessler was hard. It was emotional, and it was scary. It was like one day I was drinking and having fun with my friends, then I woke up in a hospital bed with tubes coming out of me. I remember being in a room with one of my therapists, and she was pulling up pictures of different animals for me to see if I knew what they were. As I was sitting there, she would flip the screen to a picture of a rabbit. I would sit in silence for a few seconds, look at her, and then say, "Rabbit." She would look back at me, all ecstatic, and be like, "Yessss, Dylan, good job!"

The scary thing is that I wasn't getting all of them right. There were some animals that would cross the screen and my mind would draw a blank. I wasn't necessarily guessing the wrong animal, but I would sit there in silence, look at her, and say, "I'm sorry, I can't remember."

It was such a degrading feeling. It was degrading because I would lie in bed, knowing I should obviously know that when a green animal with a shell pops on the screen, it's a turtle. Even though my brain wasn't conscious enough to know what the animal was, my brain was conscious enough to know I should be getting that right. And it affected me a lot emotionally.

My brain would shut down and I would fall asleep around 8 pm every night. I went from pulling all-nighters in college to being lights out and tucked under the covers at 8 pm. My brain was so weak that it didn't have the fortitude to do some therapy work and manage to stay functioning.

I would wake up in the morning and instantly feel like a loser. I felt like a mistake. Like I said before, I had the IQ of a third grader, but consciously I knew I should be better than that. I should be smarter than that. And I shouldn't be where I was.

I was living my life in the most unhealthy way you possibly can. And that way of living is the, "I wish I never..." mentality. Every morning I woke up and every night when I went to bed, I would say to myself, "God, I wish I never hopped on that skateboard. Imagine how simple my life would be…"

I quickly learned that you can't live your life in a state of regret. There's no magic wand that can go back in time and go, "POOF!" to just magically transform your life. Guess what? I DID hop on that skateboard. So, no matter how many times I wanted to sit back and write the script differently in my head, no matter how many times I lived a woe-is-me lifestyle, I was still going to wake up tomorrow with a traumatic brain injury! And I was still going to go to therapy! Learning basic math, learning how to walk, and learning how to APPRECIATE LIFE!

After about two weeks of being in Kessler, I got the approval to head home. I struggled to really process this. Where was home? When I get "home," what's next? It frightened me. My mom came to pick me up. I have a few mental images of being wheeled down the hallway. This one nurse that cared about me a lot cheered me on, saying, "You've got this Dylan! Go out there and get 'em!"

It's hard to really put it into words. Because, the way this story is going, it sounds like I'm all good now. It sounds like I just got released from Kessler and I'm back to normal. Wrong. VERY wrong. As I was leaving Kessler, to my mother it seemed like I was going to be living with her for the rest of my life.

The reason Kessler was releasing me was because there was only so much the hospital could do. It was costing money to stay there, and reasonably it made more sense to be home with my family. I needed to go home, have my family take care of me, and start going to therapy.

So, I made it back. I lived on the second floor of our house, but my mom had me staying in a room on the first floor. Just because I couldn't really walk yet and, well, I was in no shape to be walking upstairs. Fortunately, there was a Kessler rehab about twenty minutes from my home, so I would be going there three days a week. I couldn't drive yet, so I was being driven by my dad.

HOME

I STILL REMEMBER THE DAY I GOT HOME FROM the hospital. My mom was driving the car, and we pulled into the driveway. My father, so happy to have me home, was videoing my arrival. I couldn't get out of the car on my own, so my mom parked the car, walked over to the passenger side, and helped me out.

I was speechless. So dazed and confused. Outside the front door were all these welcome home balloons. If you watch the video my dad took, I walked right up to the balloons and just started poking them. My brain couldn't fathom what the balloons were really there for.

Neither of my siblings were in New Jersey at the time, so it was just my parents there. Looking back, it's like my brain couldn't comprehend how big of a deal it was that I made it out of the hospital. I was acting like when you see a kid at the dentist who was just given laughing gas to relieve the pain. I was so happy-go-lucky, seeing balloons and seeing Bandit (my dog), just smiling cheek-to-cheek.

One day, I got home from therapy and my mom was kind of just trying to test me and quiz me to see how bad my injury truly was. I didn't really have my phone while I was hospitalized unless my mom brought it with her when she came to see me. My mom had my phone because I was extremely reckless and was texting/calling random people at random hours. One day, I asked if I could have my phone back.

My mom went into her room and got my phone. When she came out of her room, she handed it to me and asked, "Hey, D, just out of curiosity, what's your phone number again?" I froze. I looked at her and said, "848…" and went silent.

I couldn't even remember my phone number. Naturally, people's numbers are hardwired into their subconscious minds just from having to say it or use it over and over again. But, for me, it was like everything I knew from before my injury was wiped away. It was sad. It was sad because I knew that it was something I should know, but when my mom asked me the question my mind went completely blank. It was like having to reteach a third grader. Yet that third grader was in a twenty-one year old's body.

———

I was doing physical therapy, cognitive therapy, and speech therapy. The physical therapy basically consisted of learning how to walk again. For the first two weeks, I had a walker and my therapist right by my side just in case. Next, I learned how to walk without the walker. I had a therapist with her hand on my right shoulder making sure I was okay. After about a month, I was walking side to side. You're laughing, but that was actually harder than you would think for a twenty-one-year-old athlete. And then after about two months, I worked my way up to running.

I'll never forget when I ran for the first time. My physical therapist took me out to the parking lot. We walked back and forth once. I remember the build up to running. What seems so simple to people—to just start running—held so much fear in my mind before I started. Then, holding my hand, we both started to jog. My legs felt so weak. She held onto me so tight. We went up and down the parking lot, then she let go of my hand. I was moving so slowly, but I was jogging! I looked at her smiling. "Amy! I'm running!" She was ecstatic for me. For me, it was a HUGE sigh of relief. It was reassurance that, by overcoming some of my fears, I may be able to do more than I think I can. It felt like such a big milestone.

For speech, well, I was learning how to pronounce three-syllable words and spell again. This shit was hard for me. My brain was struggling to pronounce certain words. Sam, my speech therapist, started asking me to spell words and to pronounce them. Then, I was trying to form sentences with certain words. Sam would give me three or four words. He would say to me, "Happy, park, dog, sun." And I would have to look back at him and say, "I am happy to take my dog to the park when the sun is out." It wasn't all that easy for me, though. I would hear Sam say the words, take a good ten to fifteen seconds to digest them, and look back at him while forming the sentence.

For cognitive therapy, I had a lot of work to do. This was where I took the biggest hit from my injury. My working memory was struggling the most, so I was doing a lot of short-term memory and attention work. For more detail, working memory is short-term memory and attention. David, my cognitive therapist, well, we had a bond from the start. I could genuinely feel this man's excitement when I would walk in the room. No matter how frustrating it was, he looked forward to working with me.

David not only cared about my progress, but he cared about me as a person. Even if he had a patient right after our session, he made sure to take five minutes to check in on me and to see how I was doing mentally. A lot of the work David and I did was little tests for my memory.

David would read me four words. He would say, "Car, blue, shirt, water. What was the word I said before shirt?" And, like I said, this was really hard for me.

Yet out of everything I just named, walking, working memory, spelling, pronouncing words… the hardest part of it all was being able to *accept it*. The hardest part was being happy with where I was in life. Being happy that I survived. It was difficult for me to wake up in the morning, look in the mirror, and appreciate life. Waking up in the morning and being grateful for the fact that I survived an injury that had a ninety percent chance of dying. I really didn't appreciate life and I didn't appreciate the fact that I survived an injury that seemed like I was going to die from.

A common saying that gets thrown around is, "Man, I'm struggling. I really am at rock bottom." Ironic that it was me being one of the people that used to throw that saying around. But let me tell ya, you might think you've hit rock bottom, but you'll REALLY fuckin' know when you've hit rock bottom. God. I used to say it all the time. I would fail a math test, have a bad break up with a girlfriend, play like shit in a basketball game, and be walking around town saying, "Man, I'm at rock bottom."

I'm here to tell you no, you're not. Life just got a little rough. Life's just trying to teach you some lessons. You'll really know when you're at rock bottom. When you can't remember what you had for breakfast. When you can't do seven-times-three, you'll know you're at rock bottom.

As you can imagine, you will never hear those words come out of my mouth again.

———

So, I was really struggling recovery-wise. For the first three months, October through December, I was recovering, but not a he'll-be-able-to-go-back-to-college-and-live-on-his-own type of recovering.

———

I could tell things weren't going well with my girlfriend. She didn't want anything to do with me. And I get it. I can't imagine dating someone and then out of nowhere they have the IQ of a third grader. But I could tell she didn't want a single thing to do with me.

And then she broke up with me. Didn't really give me a reason. Just told me she had a lot on her plate and she needed some time to focus on herself. It was hard for me. The time when I felt like I needed the most support, I was given the opposite. It messed with my head… a lot. And I don't want to sit here throwing shots at people for decisions made in the past. But I also don't want to forget how deeply it cut me. It definitely put a dent in me. With that being said, I also want to take note of how necessary it was for my recovery. I grew from this tremendously. And I firmly believe a different person came out from this experience. A different person with a mindset shift to work harder, love deeper, and really just grow. Nothing but gratitude for this, for it led me to where I am today.

BELIEVE

I'LL NEVER FORGET IT. I LEARNED WHY THEY use the word "traumatic" with a brain injury, because I will have moments where I'm lying in bed and I just have flashbacks to some of the suffering I went through on this journey of mine. Here is a big one that I have traumatic flashbacks of.

It resonates in my head like it was yesterday. Like I've said, I was at an extreme low. What really made it an ultimate low was that I had a brain hemorrhage in my frontal lobe. And your frontal lobe is like your emotions control center. So, my emotions were all sorts of wacked up. I would be having a good day, feeling like I'm recovering well and I'm on the right path, then twenty minutes later I would feel useless and like I was an absolute piece of shit. And then I would be depressed for two hours. And then I was giggling on the couch with my dad again about the *Schitt's Creek* episode we just watched.

But there was one night I was taking a shower. And I was all sorts of in my head. Thinking about my injury, where I was in life, and comparing myself to all my friends in college partying and having a good time. I stopped the shower and got out.

And my heart dropped.

I looked in the mirror at myself, and just felt absolutely useless. I looked at myself and I said, "Fuck you. Fuck you for surviving an injury you were supposed to die from. There was a ninety percent chance you would die, but for some reason the ten percent chance won. You are cursed."

And I truly believed I was cursed. I fully believed in curses and that I was cursed for a good two to three months. It was traumatic. And there are times when I'm in my bathroom and look in the mirror and have a flashback to that night. Although I have really grown from that time and don't believe that anymore, that trauma sticks with me.

I was never really a religious guy growing up. I had a catholic father who went to church every Sunday and a mom who never really went to church unless it was Christmas or Easter. My dad was very easy with us. He never tried to force us, and he never made it feel mandatory. Every Sunday morning, he would walk in my room and say, "Hey, D, I'm about to go to church. Do you want to come this week?"

Annoyed at his question, I would roll over in bed, "No, Dad," and he would calmly go his way. I'll never forget, one night after my injury, I was down bad thinking about all the challenges life was throwing at me. I was lying in bed and I was thinking, "Why was I the unfortunate one who fell off a skateboard and had a traumatic brain injury? People fall off skateboards every day and they never get traumatic brain injuries."

Then I was thinking, "What if I barely recover and I'm stupid and I can't ever live without my mom?!" And that's when I really broke down. That was when I couldn't help but feel useless. I felt like a loser. And I just started sobbing.

But then, for some divine reason, a voice in my head told me to get out of bed, kneel on the ground, and pray. So, I did. My bedroom lamp was on, and I was alone. It was silent in my room, you could hear a pin drop. I got out of bed, I kneeled down beside my bed, put my hands together making a cross, and I began to pray as I was fighting back tears.

"Please, God, please," I murmured under my breath. "I know I wasn't always the most religious man, and I know I didn't truly believe in you for some time. And that almost makes me feel guilty for turning to you when I need you, but not when I'm doing well. But Lord, or whatever higher power is listening to me… please, heal my brain. Improve my memory. Improve my attention. And I will have a healthier relationship with you, and I will use my recovery as a tool to share my story and help people struggling," I said with my eyes closed and my hands forcefully against my head.

Now, I'm not sitting here writing this trying to convince you what you should believe in… however, despite how bad my memory was during that time of my life, I still remember that prayer. Word for word, like it was yesterday. And I don't believe that's a coincidence. I believe that stuck with me because some sort of higher being brought it to reality, as I had a recovery that didn't seem imaginable back then, delivered just like I prayed for.

Like I said, I'm not going to sit here and tell you what to believe in or who to believe in. But I will tell you to *believe in something*. Someone put you on this earth for a reason. Believe that, and believe that you are worthy of making a difference in this world.

Having a spiritual connection will give you a shoulder to lean on when times get hard. Having a religion to follow will give this life you live some meaning and some purpose. A religion can help you find some clarity in this whirlwind of a life we live.

SUNSHINE STATE

BOTH MY PARENTS ARE RETIRED, AND BEFORE my injury happened, they had rented a condo in Florida for three months in the winter. They rented the condo for February, March, and April. However, when my injury happened, they weren't planning on going. They thought it was good for me to stay in Jersey doing therapy at Kessler because that was the only therapy we knew.

Since my emotions were all out of line, I was going to a clinical therapist to talk about how I was feeling. It was about two months after my injury, so I was still extremely shaken up trying to grasp how this could be reality. When I told him how I felt guilty that my parents were supposed to go to Florida, but weren't going because of me, he said we should be going to Florida. He said there was a good TBI (traumatic brain injury) therapy in Florida called Saint Mary's Hospital. He also said that the weather and change of scenery would be good for me emotionally.

So, that's what we did. We packed up the bags and went to Florida for two months. The doctors were still hesitant about me being on a plane, so we drove. We were in the car for eight hours and decided to make a pit stop in Charleston for two nights. We thought it would be a good idea to split the drive in half and get me to see some of my friends. But, the truth is, it ended up making things harder for me.

I was a new person. I was living a different life now. I was a different person walking into my house at 23 Amherst Street than I was the last time I walked out. And that was hard for me to accept. I remember my mom got a hotel room on Calhoun Street and I was staying at my house the first night we got to Charleston. Around 11 pm, my mom got a phone call…

"I can't stay here, mom. I can't do this. I'm looking at everything in this room and I just feel like that was a different life than the life I'm living now," I told her as tears began to run down my face. I was looking around my room at posters and flags that felt like a different person used to own. I was trying to balance the old me with the new me, while maintaining the feelings of being lost and confused. "Okay, D, that's okay. I'll come pick you up," my mom told me. And that was exactly what I needed. Comfort. I needed to know that it was okay that I felt that way. So, I went and stayed with my mom at the hotel.

The next night was a very special night for me. And it was a night that I will never forget. All of my friends knew I was back in town and made plans to go to Fuel to all get dinner together.

Now that I can look back with more understanding of how emotional that time period was for everyone, there was so much love at that dinner table. I had a few friends canceling plans to be there and a few friends skipping class to be there. And I would never expect them to do that.

They did that out of brotherhood. They did that out of love. No matter what was going on in the world, they would have dropped it in a heartbeat to be there. And I'll never be able to show as much appreciation as that moment holds in my heart.

The next morning, my mom and I woke up bright and early and hit the road. As we left Charleston, it was hard for me. I remember my mind was running a mile a minute. It was almost like I got a taste of what my life was supposed to be like and then got it yanked away from me. Almost like a reminder from God saying, "Sorry, Dylan, this is what your life is supposed to look like, but it's not." But I tried to redirect my mind. Florida was next. Focus on Florida. This is going to help me heal.

And my therapist was right. The weather helped me out so much. Being able to wake up every morning to eighty-degree sunny weather improved my emotions so much. I was able to find joy in other aspects of life other than just dwelling on a brain injury and therapy. It was so nice being in Florida, and having a different therapist look at my injury was huge. I'll never forget my therapist, Lara.

The therapy was different in Florida. But different in a better way. Whereas in New Jersey I had three different therapists—one each for cognitive, speech, and physical—I now had only one therapist. And she was doing both cognitive and speech.

My physical abilities recovered rather quickly. As I left

New Jersey, my physical therapist, Amy, gave me the all-clear. She told me I was walking fine, I was running fine, and I would no longer need it. Prior to this, I was getting so used to negativity occurring in my life. So, being able to get positive feedback was such a much needed uplift in my life. It helped me realize I am capable of turning things around and moving in the right direction.

So, now it was Lara and me working on my speech and cognitive skills. And I loved Lara. She was helping me so much. For my memory, instead of using worksheets, she was more so using real life examples.

For example, at the end of the day, she asked me to tell my mom everything I did that day. She wanted me to do it in full detail, too. For example, instead of saying, "I went to therapy and then got coffee," saying, "I went to therapy, we did memory worksheets where she would read me a story and then at the end ask a detailed question about something specific, that was so small I might have missed it unless I paid full attention to her story, and then I went to Perk and got a black coffee." So, it was the same sentence, just in more detail. This way, it was forcing me to use my memory and attention throughout the day instead of just in one hour of therapy.

It was a turning point for my recovery. Being in Florida helped me a lot. It was like a breath of fresh air that was very much needed. The weather was seventy-five degrees and sunny every day and the condo had a nice pool area with a dock where I could kayak. I made a friend named David while I was there, and it was nice because he had no previous Dylan to compare me to at all. David was only a year younger than me, and he liked me for me. We kayaked, fished, and just had a good time. I really learned how to take a step to the side of all that I was going through and really enjoy being in the moment. Not living life talking about the past, but instead being present and just living in the now.

I even joined my mom's pickleball league, playing at 8 am every morning. The league consisted of retired couples ages fifty-five and older, and then me sitting in at twenty-one years old. They loved it. And I loved it, too. I was someone new for them, some young life added to the mix. And the truth was the majority of them were better than me. Some of them had game.

It was important for me to feel accepted into a group. Before you start laughing, since they're retired older men and women, it was crucial for me to work on who I was post injury. I felt love, competition, and really just good memories from strangers that soon became friends.

ACCEPTANCE

I DID STILL FIND MYSELF DEALING WITH SE-vere depression. Although I had more distractions to pull me away from it, when I was in solitude I found myself battling some demons. Some demons that had good leverage on me. Some demons that knew my weak spots, and they knew it well.

I was sad. I still felt like a mistake. I still found myself asking the world, "Why me?" I still found myself asking, "Is this real life? Why does this happen to people? Not even why does this happen to people, why did this happen to me?"

But I kept pushing. I found myself going to the gym every day. Some days I was going twice. I would finish a set, look at myself in the mirror, and say to myself, "You left Charleston as the kid with a brain injury and you're gonna come back looking like a different person." Sounds cheesy, but my goal was to just grow as a person. My goal was for people to be shocked. For people to be confused from what they're hearing from other people and what they're now seeing.

I saw this article that absolutely redirected my thought process. What it said was, when times get hard, you need to become best friends with your pain. Instead of saying, "Boo-hoo I feel bad for myself," wake up in the morning and say, "Today's not going to be easy. I might struggle today, but I will learn from you. And I will become better and stronger from you. Thank you, pain. For you are making me a stronger man."

So, that's what I did. I would wake up in the morning looking forward to growing from the pain I was going through. I would accept where I was in life and try to grow from it. For when I wasn't accepting of where I was in life, it was only making it harder. It wasn't changing anything.

I learned that there is a difference between pain and suffering. Pain is inevitable. Pain teaches you how to get somewhere in life. It gives you obstacles and challenges to get from where you are now to where you want to be. Pain is temporary. And on the other side of that pain is another version of yourself.

Suffering is letting that pain take ownership of you. Suffering is staying in a relationship that you know no longer suits your best interest. Suffering is staying at a job that is a time loop making no progress on your goals in life. There is nothing wrong with pain because it helps you grow, and makes you truly appreciate when life works in your favor. But suffering is a choice.

Pain is unavoidable. And the ironic thing is, when you try to avoid it, that is when it becomes suffering. Because the pain isn't going to disappear. I didn't choose to suffer.

But I accepted the pain I was going through, became friends with it, and grew from it.

Any ego I had, I dropped it. I didn't really have a choice. I had to accept where I was in life and by accepting it, that was the only way to grow from it. The pain taught me a work ethic that had no choice but to barrel through it. And this led to tremendous growth for me. Both physically and mentally.

I was also doing therapy homework every night. Every. Fucking. Night. I'm not kidding when I say that. Whether it was a Monday or a Friday, my mom and I would be sitting on the couch watching TV. It was usually a Knicks game or college basketball, and when it would go to commercial break, my mom would start quizzing me. We would switch up worksheets and it would be three to five minutes of her testing me on memory worksheets, then we'd get back to watching the basketball game.

Oh yeah, and of course we were mixing in a few Scrabble games, of course. Who knew I'd like Scrabble? One night, we were sitting on the couch, and there was nothing on TV. I looked over to my right to see my mom playing a game. "What's that you're playing?" I asked out of pure boredom. "This is Scrabble," my mom said back to me. With truly zero interest in the game, I said back to her, "Can I play with you?" And this interaction led to Scrabble games that are still being played to this day. For such a basic game, I truly believe this game helped my brain recover. The cognitive skill it took for me to form words off of previous words was hard for my brain back in Florida. It forced me to figure out what I can do with only a certain number of letters. Kind of like my life at the moment. Having to accept the cards life handed me, use what I can gather, and find a way to best play this game of life.

I will forever be grateful for Florida. From the therapy to the heaven-sent weather and the great people I met, it all helped me grow. I left Florida a different man than when I got there. I made great progress, but here's the thing with a severe traumatic brain injury. A great recovery doesn't mean you're done. I made progress, but there was still a lot of work that needed to be done.

FLIPPING THE SCRIPT

WHEN I GOT BACK TO NEW JERSEY, I WAS NO-where near reaching a full recovery. My working memory was really struggling, my ability to process information was struggling, and my ability to multitask was horrible. But worse than all of this, I was still insanely depressed.

And then I found out Mt. Joy was playing in Charleston on May 18. Just to refresh your memory, Mt. Joy was the concert I was at in Asheville when my injury happened. It was like a sign from God. Mt. Joy was coming to play in the city I went to school in. Not only that, but coming to the city I went to school in five days after my birthday. I knew I had to make a trip down to get my redemption. My chance to make a comeback on the severity of nearly dying when I saw them.

But the idea scared me. I really associated Mt. Joy with nearly dying, and it held a weird feeling in my body. It held a weird feeling in my body, a feeling of anxiety mixed with nervousness, but I bought my ticket and made the trip anyway, determined to overcome what felt like a milestone in my life.

The whole flight down, I was anxious. I was reliving the weekend in Asheville on repeat. Why would I do this to myself? Why would I want to rewatch the band I nearly died listening to? Stop it, Dylan. You love Mt. Joy. They were your favorite band. You have to do this. So, I made the trip.

In plain English, the whole trip was a shit show. Truly, there are no words more fitting than that. From the date my injury happened to my arrival in Charleston, there really was not a single occasion where I drank any alcohol. Nothing. Now that I think about it, there were two times I had a buddy visit me in Florida when I was doing therapy and we went out to dinner having two or three beers, but nothing ever more than that.

Then I arrived in Charleston for my birthday weekend and the Mt. Joy concert, and the booze just started to flow. It was so many people's first time seeing me since my injury, so out of excitement in seeing me, endless people were buying me shots and beers. I mean, it was all out of love, but it almost seems like common sense that maybe it isn't the best idea to be buying the guy with a fresh brain injury a shot of tequila.

Here's the thing, I have enough accountability to not put the blame on them. I mean, let's be honest, if I was smart enough, I could have said no. It sounds pretty understandable if someone were to buy me a beer and I say, "I appreciate that so much but with my injury I really shouldn't drink more than four or five," and just like that, they'd probably say, "Damn, your loss, more for me," and walk away.

But I didn't do that. I drank like a fish for three days straight. Being fresh off a brain injury, the alcohol didn't mix too well. With the anxiety I had about seeing Mt. Joy and the three consecutive bad nights I had, I was in a very bad place mentally.

The idea of seeing them was scaring me so much that the morning of the concert I woke up at 4 am, called my mom, and said, "I don't think I can do this, mom." I said, "I need to leave here, I can't see the band I nearly died listening to." And I left. I changed my flight, and I went home.

Like I said earlier, I had full-on convinced myself that I was not supposed to survive that accident. I would wake up in the morning, look in the mirror, and hate who was looking back. What I saw looking back at me was a kid who wasn't supposed to survive a catastrophic injury. I saw a kid who could barely remember what he had for dinner last night. I saw a kid looking back who had the IQ of a third grader. I walked around with a negative attitude and acted like everything that happened to me was horrible.

I haven't told many people about this phase mostly because it's something I don't enjoy talking about, but I went through a serious suicidal phase. One thing I'm grateful for is that I never had it in me to hurt myself. The main reason being my mom. I knew how hard it had hurt my mom as she watched a kid she birthed nearly die. And I beat myself up for this every day. The amount of stress and anxiety I put this lady through, I would never forgive myself. So, now that she had a little ray of hope that I survived, I could never hurt her even more by killing myself. That lady was too strong for me to show that I'm that weak.

But then I reached my breaking point.

One night, my sister was driving me to a friend's house when I let it loose. I was really messed up in the head, and times were hard. I believe it was Memorial Day weekend or the first week of June. Once we got to the kid's house, I said to Kelli, "How sad would it be if I survived an injury that had a ninety percent death rate, had doctors calling me 'Miracle Man,' and then I committed suicide?" My sister went silent. I gave her about fifteen seconds to say something and she couldn't get a word out. So, I got out of the car and went to my friend's house.

About ten minutes into being at my friend's, my mom called me. I clicked ignore. Then again my mom started calling. So, I answered the phone and walked out of the room. She said, "I'm on my way, Kelli told me what happened, we're going to the hospital." Looking back, to show how badly I needed to go to the hospital, I didn't even argue with her. I said, "Okay," and hung up the phone. My mom picked me up and we went to the hospital.

It was at that moment everything turned around for me.

I was lying in a hospital bed, the doctor talking to my mom about possibly putting me in a psych ward, when I realized, what's wrong with you? You've been telling yourself it's a curse that the ten percent chance of surviving won, when really you're a damn blessing. I was lying in that hospital bed when it hit me.

If there's such a thing as a holy spirit, then that's what took control of me. In my head, my whole narrative I was writing about my life flipped perspective. It absolutely transformed right here at this moment. I was changed.

I've never loved life more than this moment where I'm at now. I'm a damn walking miracle and I will never look at life through the lens I was before this.

And that was it. I went to that hospital suicidal, and I left more appreciative of life than I ever was before. I needed that wake-up call. Every breath you take, be grateful for that. Because someone wasn't as lucky as you are today.

I wanted to make the most of every second I could now. Whether it was with my family, with my friends, or even at therapy, I wanted to work as hard as I possibly could. And I was. To this day, my mom says she noticed the change in me. The doctors wanted to put me on anti-depressants and medications to avoid that suicidal thought process I was having. I told them I didn't need medication. I had the best medication of them all, and that medication was life.

Life... being able to wake up in the morning and hear the birds chirping. Rolling out of bed to a beautiful sunrise coming over the trees. Walking downstairs and hearing my dad laughing. It was like a new world I was living in. It's crazy how, when you change your perspective, you change your whole reality.

For example, "I have to watch my sister's play Friday night," versus, "I get to watch my sister's play Friday night."

It's as simple as changing your vocab, and your whole perspective changes along with it.

I registered to go back to college in Charleston for the fall semester and worked my ass off to try and get there because there were still things to do before I left. And I did it! I made it back to Charleston.

BACK AT COLLEGE

MY PSYCHIATRIST TOLD ME I SHOULD ONLY register for three classes because it might be difficult for me to retain information with my working memory issues. I said, "No, I can handle four." I knew taking four would push me harder to focus and be the best student I could possibly be. This lady that works for Charleston told me, "When you fail a class, just know your psychiatrist said you should only take three."

That was exactly what I needed to hear. It FIRED me up! The second I heard that, I KNEW I wasn't failing a class. When I know there is someone out there doubting me, someone out there doubting what I am capable of, that fuels me to do even better. She didn't even say, "If you fail a class." She said, "When." That shit stuck with me.

By the way, I didn't fail a class.

I was so grateful to be back in Charleston. It's so funny looking back now, because most people dread when that time of the week comes when they HAVE to do laundry. They HAVE to fold all the clothes. They HAVE to put it all away. But, since I was so excited to just be back in

Charleston, living on my own, I would get excited to do my laundry! It sounds crazy, but I remember it made me feel SO self-sufficient. It made me feel independent, that I was moving in the right direction.

In December of 2020, they were asking me which sibling I could live with and what hobbies I had that could keep me busy for the rest of my life. By August of 2021, I was living on my own, living the lifestyle of a college student again. These thoughts went through my head as I did my laundry, smiling. It felt absolutely unreal. I was like a five-year-old on Christmas morning grinning cheek-to-cheek. Just walking to class felt better than it ever did.

I did have my academic struggles, though. As I have said, my memory did not recover one hundred percent. I was struggling to retain some information. Since I was a Hospitality and Tourism major, I had to fulfill my business credits. I took financial accounting sophomore year, but I still had to take my managerial accounting course.

This class was definitely difficult for my memory. It consisted of a lot of memorizing accounts and formulas. Thankfully, the College of Charleston has a program called SNAP. SNAP was a program for students with disabilities. If you were considered a SNAP student, you were given some accommodation for your disabilities. Since my disabilities were mostly memory related, I got some extended time for tests, and the professor would share class notes with me after class. I was appreciative of the extra support because it was guidance like that which made a huge difference.

Before my injury, I was enrolled in a managerial accounting class. However, due to my injury, I had to drop all my classes. Once I felt like this class was going to be difficult for me, I shared my SNAP accommodations with my professor and reminded him about my injury.

He emailed me back saying, "Dylan... I remember your injury like it was yesterday. I had students telling me they needed some extra time to take an exam because they were struggling emotionally because of your injury. And not only was your recovery amazing, but also the fact that you are registered for my class again has me speechless. Anything I can do to accommodate you, please let me know. God bless you."

The class did not come easily to me, but with some hard work and some help from my professor, I passed the class. I had a few other courses that were not easy for me. But, like I've said, I viewed school differently than I did before my injury. I was blessed to have the opportunity to learn in a classroom, and that made me work harder than I ever did before. And although the classes weren't always fun, I worked my ass off to get my degree.

MENTORSHIP

THE SEMESTER AFTER MY INJURY, OUR SCHOOL gym only allowed twenty percent capacity in the gym because of COVID-19 regulations, so I was going to Gold's Gym in Mount Pleasant. I was consistently going with my friend Chris around 8-9 am every morning.

One morning, while we were working out, I noticed this man wearing a shirt that said, "Being comfortable and common sucks!" During my recovery, I went on a hunt for motivational speakers to keep my head up, and during the journey I discovered David Goggins. Goggins used to always call himself, "uncommon amongst uncommon people," and that aligned with me very well. After all I had been through, I felt like I was uncommon amongst uncommon people. It's uncommon for people to have a brain injury, and it is all the more uncommon to have a recovery and perspective flip like I did.

So, when I saw this guy's shirt, some spark went off in my head that I had to say something to him about how I liked his shirt. So, I went up to him, and I told him that

I liked his shirt. He said, "Thank you," and we went our separate ways.

As my day went on, I couldn't stop thinking about the brief interaction I had with this man. I wanted that shirt so bad. So, I looked it up on Google: *Being comfortable and common sucks!* But nothing came up. Next, I searched *Shirts about being uncommon*. Again, nothing came up.

I was so confused. I told myself, if I happened to see this guy at the gym again, I'd ask him where I can get that shirt. It fit my mentality too well to not ask where I could get that.

The next day I saw him. I walked right up to the man and I asked him, "I really liked that shirt you were wearing the other day. Where can I get a shirt like that? I looked it up but couldn't find it."

His face lit up with a big smile. "I appreciate that so much, man," he said back to me. "The reason it's hard to find the shirt is because that's my own company. I can get one shipped here and I'll bring it in for you by next week," the man told me. I was so happy! This guy was way too cool and too nice to be giving a kid he doesn't even know a shirt.

The next Monday, the man approached me at Gold's. He handed me the shirt. "I appreciate this so much, man," I told the guy. "Can I give you some money? This is awesome!" He laughed at me.

"No, no, you don't have to give me any money. My name's Paul, by the way," he said and gave me a handshake. "You seem like a hard working dude, and you have a similar mindset if you came up to me and told me you liked my shirt. What's your phone number?" Paul asked me.

I gave him my phone number and he proceeded to tell me, "I'm a firm believer in giving back. For me, I had a mentor in my life that redirected my path and helped me get where I am today. If you want mentorship and some guidance, you're more than welcome to come over, cost-free, and learn a thing or two," Paul told me.

This didn't seem real. "Of course, I would do that! That sounds amazing!" I told him. "We'll stay in touch and work out a time and date. Keep getting after it, brother," he said, gave me a handshake, and walked away.

I would meet with Paul in between my college classes once a month. This went on for about eight months straight. Paul helped me with everything from financial advice, career advice, spiritual advice, and everything in between. To this day, anytime I need someone to turn to, Paul is the first person I text. Paul has guided me in ways I couldn't have imagined.

It was a chance encounter that changed my life. And that is where I don't believe in coincidences. I believe God placed him on my journey for us to cross paths. It has now been over two years, and Paul still fits me in his crazy schedule if I text him seeing if we can meet. And honestly, I wouldn't have built up the mental fortitude to be sitting here writing this book if it wasn't for his guidance.

Paul saw my vision and he knew I wanted to inspire and impact people with my story. Whether it was public speaking, working in hospitals, doing in-patient therapy, or anywhere in between. He told me the first step for getting my story out was writing a book. And the idea terrified me at first. But I looked up to Paul like a role model, and I trusted his guidance. So, I started writing. I thought, let me get my story on paper and see how it goes. And the truth is, it really just flowed effortlessly. Since this was such a traumatic and life changing time period for me, it really just came straight from my heart. And it felt good, too. It felt good to get all my thoughts and emotions on paper. When I started writing, I would tell myself, if someday I get one person to reach out to me and tell me that sharing my experience helped them, that would be all I need to feel like an impact.

Paul and I doing teatime at one of our mentorship meetings

So, I do take pride in the ways I have changed. I know that sounds crazy, but it almost feels like parts of me that I didn't like died off with my injury, and new parts emerged. The truth is, I wouldn't change a thing about the struggles I went through. I love the way I evolved from this experience. And when times get hard, you really do get to see people's true colors. I love the life I lived before my injury, but I love even more the man I have become from it. I learned discipline, how to love who I am, injury or no injury, and, most importantly, turning hardships into blessings.

IF YOU ARE SCARED TO JUMP, YOU JUMP!

OH YEAH, IT GETS BETTER. I MET A GORGEOUS girl that went to Charleston. I still remember the second I laid my eyes on her, as I felt a connection I've never really felt before. It was an amazing feeling. Yet, I was terrified at the same time. It's one of those feelings you can't even explain, it just leaves you speechless.

Eva was such a big part of my recovery. Well, I did the work for the therapy and the healing, but Eva was really what I needed to help me feel comfortable in my own shoes and build some confidence in who I was. Eva saw me for who I am—accepted that I had a catastrophic injury and wasn't going to be living life the same as a lot of these other college guys she knew. While Eva didn't know the inner work I was doing to feel accepted and confident in this new person I was becoming, her openness to communicate and show me feelings of worth led to so much for me.

We hit things off rather fast, but I was still extremely insecure about my injury because my circumstances were different from the average guy she knew. I told her I had short-term memory problems. I told her I had attention problems. And I also let her know I couldn't really drink or party like all the other guys. I told her I planned on never having a girlfriend again just because I was scarred by things that had happened in the past and I wanted nothing too serious. She agreed and we just wanted to have fun. But it doesn't really work like that.

Over time, I caught feelings. She was awesome and understanding of my problems from my injury. She was amazed by my story and who I was, and it actually attracted her even more. She thought it wasn't realistic that someone could be in a coma and come back with such positivity and optimism. I was so confused. I wasn't expecting a girl to view my injury like this. But it was true. We really hit it off and have an amazing connection.

From my injury, I did have some problems that I was scared of, but Eva was so understanding about it all. Instead, she actually loved that I was different, and I wasn't expecting that either. For the longest time, I viewed my injury as something that would hold me back in life. Meanwhile, this girl was acting like I was capable of so much because of it.

Like I said earlier, I never wanted to be in a relationship again. My trust was just all out of line, and I didn't want to risk having someone leave me again. And even though this girl was giving me every reason in the world to ask her out, it was almost like I was looking for something to go wrong. But, instead, we just had three months of amazing memories. And that was when it hit me. I can't live my life fearing past events when I could be excited for new opportunities.

This girl has given me zero reason to push things off any longer. So, I did. November 28, 2021, I asked Eva to be my girlfriend. I'm so grateful that I did. I overcame a fear that I had, and I opened a door full of such amazing memories. When you're most scared to jump, is exactly when you should jump. And that's what I did. I jumped, and it led to so much growth for me.

Eva Mai, you inspired me to fulfill my purpose and take pride in the fact that I'm different.

GRADUATION

I MISSED A FULL YEAR OF COLLEGE, SO I WAS A year behind my friends and classmates. However, when I was in high school, I was in this academy Manasquan High School offered called the Academy of Finance. I took four classes that I got twelve college credits for while in high school. I also took two to three college courses in the summer of my freshman going into sophomore year. So, between the twelve credits I got in high school and the summer courses I took, I was only twelve credits away from graduating with my class.

I approached my advisor, telling him how I wished I could walk with my friends and how I was only twelve credits behind. He told me that since I was so close to graduating on time, and the reason I wasn't going to walk was because of a medical reason, that I was allowed to walk in graduation. Of course, I still had four more classes to take the upcoming fall, but I was allowed to walk in this graduation beforehand.

It was an amazing feeling. I was able to walk with all of my friends, my girlfriend, and, most importantly, have my family sitting in the crowd. It was a really special moment for me. As I walked across that stage, what was really thirty seconds felt like hours in my head. I was replaying in my head the doctors telling me I would never graduate college and might have to live with a sibling the rest of my life. I really did defy all odds.

All those hard moments led to this moment right here. All the nights lying in bed, staring at the ceiling with depressive thoughts running through my head. The days in therapy learning basic math and pronouncing three-syllable words. The days at Kessler Institute holding onto handlebars as I struggled to learn how to walk again. They all led to this moment right here, looking out across the Cistern yard at my mom and dad standing, hooting and hollering. Turning back to my friends in their white tuxedos, standing and clapping. This moment right here was what all those hard, sad, and scary moments led to. I am so grateful to all the people that helped me throughout this experience.

So, here's the truth. There's got to be a reason why the ten percent chance of surviving won. I don't believe in luck anymore. I don't believe I just got lucky, and I was one of the rare ones who made it. I believe I was left here for a reason. I was left here for a purpose.

And I believe that purpose was to teach, inspire, and change people's lives. Teach people that there is no easy way to go through life. Whether you like it or not, life is going to get hard. I believe my purpose is to teach people healthy ways to approach life when it gets tough. I had some incredibly hard challenges. Some moments when I really handled it in an unhealthy way and wanted to end it all. I'll show you some ways that helped me find my purpose and live life a healthy and happy way.

Walking at Graduation on May 7, 2022

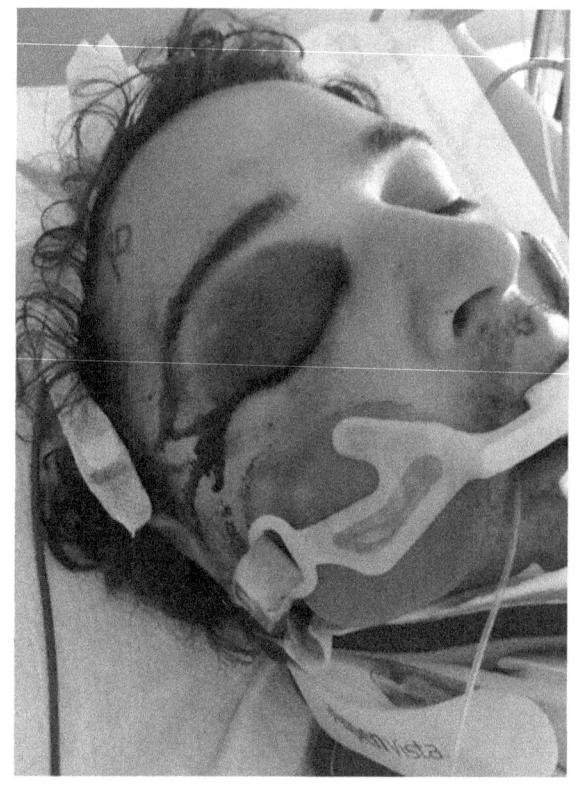

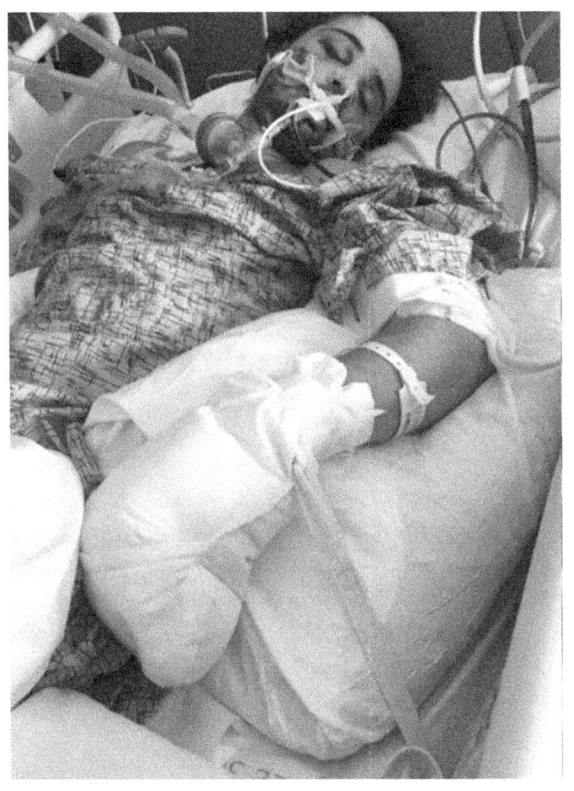

PART 3
LESSONS LEARNED &
POSITIVE LIFESTYLE HABITS

As I began my road to recovery, I wanted to learn more about the mind. I began reading and researching more and this led to ways of growth that couldn't even be predicted. I wanted to share with you some of what I learned so you can apply some of these lessons to your life.

As I have found interest in all of these lessons, I hope you do, too.

THE MIND

"The mind is everything. What you think, you become."
- Buddha

I'M GOING TO START OFF BY SAYING THE MOST important unknown fact, and it's that your mind has infinite power. You don't even know what your mind is capable of, and yet here's what's crazy. It's simple.

What you feed your mind, you get in return. If you feed your mind shit, you're going to attract shit. When I say this, I mean the way you talk to yourself. For example, if you walk in the door and the first thing you say to your mom is, "I had the worst day. I got in a fight with Charlie, and it rained all day. And then we had to go to the third grade play. It was so stupid. Today sucked." Guess what? Tomorrow's probably going to suck, too.

By saying this stuff to yourself, you're programming your mind for "things that suck." You're training your mind to focus on the negative. If you focus on what sucked, if you focus on what was hard, you're attracting more hard stuff in your life. For example, if you don't bother to study for a test because it's going to be hard either way, it's not going to help improve your grade. Your grade will not be better by not studying.

However, when you put in the work necessary, and you believe you are going in prepared, you are setting yourself up for success.

Your mind works in a very simple manner. It attracts what it is fed. When I learned this, I didn't fully believe it. So, I gave it a try. I read this article and it said when you wake up in the morning, you need to journal three things you're grateful for.

The reason is because when you first wake up, your mind switches from delta waves to theta waves. Theta waves occur during a daydream state when you're first waking up and really becoming present. The brain then moves to alpha waves when you are awake, but you are not fully processing much yet. So, by journaling three things you're grateful for, your mind is focusing on the positivity in life and not thinking about the negative.

By doing this, you are now training your brain. Jay Shetty, author and life coach, taught me that we should only use words that are pleasing and don't agitate the minds of others. So, you are training your brain to focus on the good in life and to weed out the negative. You will naturally begin to attract the good in life. You are looking at situations and trying to find the positive. For example, some people see a bee and their first reaction is, "Oh no! I don't want to get stung!" and they get alarmed. But if your mind is focusing on the positive, you look at a bee and think,

"Wow, isn't it crazy. That little bee produces such valuable honey." It's finding the positive in situations. It's also about maintaining calmness.

Now, of course, your brain might still be conscious of getting stung. However, now it is more appreciative of the good things in life opposed to just focusing on the bad. If you face the fear with calmness and mental clarity, it changes your approach to how you go about life. *Program your mind for a positive life.*

CONSCIOUS VS.
SUBCONSCIOUS MIND

"All problems are illusions of the mind"
- Eckhart Tolle

THE MIND CONSISTS OF TWO PARTS. ONE half is your conscious mind, and the other half is your subconscious mind. Your conscious mind is the part of your mind that is driving the car. The conscious mind makes the decisions and accepts what you feed it. Your conscious mind consists of your five senses: taste, hear, smell, see, and touch. Your conscious mind is also your thoughts, opinions, and beliefs.

This excerpt from David Curren (et al.) "Understand the difference between conscious and subconscious mind." is a great explanation:

"Your conscious mind is your thinking mind, and it's here where all the information received from your outside world enters. Your conscious mind makes the judgment to allow or deny the concept of entering your subconscious mind. Imagine it like a filtration system, and once the conscious mind accepts the

information, it's stored into the subconscious. Ideas, thoughts, imagination and creativity are all composed in your conscious mind.

The subconscious mind takes the responsibility of your essential life functions, fight or flight response, learned behavior and habits, memories and emotions, and 90% of all your processes and reactions occur at the subconscious level. The subconscious is involved with the storage of your experiences and knowledge and forms your dreams and nightmares. We don't think about these things, they automatically occur.

For the most part, your subconscious mind helps you navigate the world effectively, but sometimes you develop negative attitudes which hinder you from achieving your goals and raises stress. It's where more conscious thinking can benefit you because it controls your higher thinking where you can be more mindful and consider what we think, believe or act."

An interesting fact is your subconscious mind does not know the difference between the truth and a lie. It believes whatever your conscious mind feeds it. Whatever the conclusion is in your conscious mind, the subconscious accepts.

So, you think with your conscious mind, and whatever you constantly think about sinks into your subconscious mind, which then creates reality according to the nature of your thoughts. Your subconscious mind consists of your emotions and your creativity. If you think good, you attract good. If you think negatively, negativity will follow.

Something important to know is once the subconscious mind accepts an idea, it begins to make it a reality. This can be the cause of failure, loss, and unhappiness. With that being said, it can also be the cause of success, happiness, and prosperity. The mind acts upon what you feed it.

Feed your mind what you want in your reality. It is important to know that you are in control of that. And if you can control it, you can watch your life transform for the better.

STRUGGLE AND APPRECIATION

"Strength and growth come only through continuous effort and struggle"
- Napoleon Hill

NOW THIS IS ONE OF MY FAVORITE SUBJECTS to touch on. Struggle. Struggling is never fun, It's hard, frustrating, and really just a pain in the ass. As I've said, I was really struggling. But I learned a few things about struggle.

Struggle can be one of the best teachers in life. Struggle teaches you discipline. The way I like to define discipline is doing stuff you don't want to do, but doing it because you know it will benefit you in the end. Discipline is ignoring current pleasures for better long-term goals.

I became so disciplined, whether it was going to the gym, doing therapy homework, or just taking care of my body and going to bed at a reasonable hour.

For example, I had so many nights when I would want to just watch some basketball and just relax, but I knew it was in my best interest to be spending commercial breaks doing therapy work. I ignored the current pleasure of putting my feet up and relaxing to enjoy the long-term goal of having a better recovery.

If you accept struggle, it goes so much better than you think. By accepting struggle, it almost drowns the idea of it being a struggle you're having. Because once it's accepted and you're living with it by doing what you must to overcome it, it isn't so much of a struggle. It becomes a process.

The process begins when you attempt to climb the ladder. The ladder of growing from your struggle. Realizing that life is happening *for* you, and not *to* you. Working your way up so that you look back and find that struggle was necessary in getting you where you are meant to be.

It would be easy for me to look at my injury as something that happened *to* me. However, when I shifted my mindset to view my injury as something that happened *for* me, it made my whole approach to life completely different.

I was now approaching my life knowing this happened to me because I have a higher calling. A calling to overcome these struggles and challenges that life is handing me. And then while I do so, I learn and grow in a direction that can inspire and impact people with how to handle their problems.

Look at how my ladder unfolded. I was struggling. I had a TBI and I had to start from ground zero. The first step of the ladder was learning how to walk again. After I learned how to walk, I learned how to jog. After I learned how to jog, I learned how to run. This was all a step-by-step process. But if I never struggled learning how to walk first, I never would have gotten to the step on the ladder where I was running.

While it's important to have a vision of the finish line, it is important to take it step by step. And not only that, but to *enjoy* it while doing it. It's important to view your life as a ladder, as you can't just sprint to the finish line, but you can incrementally improve who you are and get to where you want to go.

And lastly, struggle teaches you to really appreciate when things are good. Struggle teaches you to open your eyes and enjoy the moment when life throws something good your way. Even the little things like a sunset, a good home-cooked meal, or a loving hug. It's like yin and yang, where the struggle you went through is necessary to really enjoy when you are not struggling. Really just appreciate it. Because you know what it feels like to struggle, and it doesn't feel as good.

THE JOURNEY

"The man who loves walking, will walk further than the man who loves the destination."

-John Moir

THIS IS ONE OF MY FAVORITE QUOTES THAT helped get me through my recovery. Let me break it down for you. If you live by this quote, how does it change your life? For me, you have learned to love the journey. When you love the journey, success just starts happening along the way.

The first few months, I really just loved the idea of reaching the destination. I just wanted to get back to being the same old Dylan. Going out, having fun, and blending in with the social crowd. For me, the destination was a full recovery. Being back in college, being able to socialize and go out, and really just being normal again.

I made progress thinking like this, but once I fell in love with the journey, EVERYTHING changed.

For me, the journey was waking up at 6 am, going to the gym, coming home, and taking a cold shower. Getting out of the shower and then going to therapy for three hours. Now, don't get me wrong, I didn't naturally love this.

But over routine and habit of doing it every day, I would wake up and put a smile on my face. I'd say to myself, "Today we're going to go to therapy and walk out of there better than when we walked in." I believed this. I transferred the thought from my conscious mind to my subconscious mind and made it reality.

So, I fell in love with my journey. For me, my journey was every step of the ladder. It was the micro habits of getting up early and maintaining discipline to get me where I wanted to go. And I walked further than when I only had the destination in mind. It's as simple as rewiring your thoughts to help get you where you want to go. Fall in love with the process. When you fall in love with the process, the goals just start to happen.

I GET VS. I HAVE

"Success is about taking advantage of opportunity"
-Mike Ditka

IT'S IMPORTANT TO WATCH THE WAY WE TALK to ourselves. It can be as simple as saying, "I get," or, "I have." When you wake up at 7 in the morning to go to school, you're tired and groggy, and you look in the mirror and say, "Ugh, I have to go to school today," it automatically puts your mind in a bad place. It puts you in a place of knowing that you're doing something you don't want to do.

If you don't really love school, it's natural to wake up and say/think, "Ugh, I have to go to school today." Now, if you change the way you word things, and you wake up and say, "I get to go to school today," it completely changes your mindset. Now your mind is interpreting going to school as an opportunity. When you're saying, "I have to go to school," your mind is interpreting it as something you are being forced to do.

Or if you need to lose some weight and you look in the mirror and say, "I get to go to the gym today," it is putting your mind into a better perspective. It is shifting your mind in the place of seeing a positive opportunity. If you say, "I have to go to the gym today," your mind is going to dread the idea of it. It really comes down to how you talk to yourself. The way you talk to yourself changes everything.

Practicing your vocab switch of "I get to" can transform your life. Replacing negative words in your vocab with more subtle words will lessen the intense emotions your brain will associate with it. Attaching your uplifting, positive words with outcomes and circumstances will lift up your mood.

EXERCISE

"If it doesn't challenge you, it won't change you."
- Fred Devito

THIS WAS A BIG ONE THAT HELPED MY RECOVery. It started because I really had NOTHING to do with my free time. So, I began going to the gym. My emotional therapist thought it might be good for me as long as I was careful and had my physiatrist approve of it. I got the yes from my physiatrist, and my fitness journey began.

I started off only going to the gym for, like, thirty minutes. Well, if you talk to my mom, she'll say it was more like ten to fifteen minutes, but I'll give myself some wiggle room.

It was painful for me to enjoy it. It was time I could have spent relaxing. It was hard work to not be seeing instant gratification. But I learned a few things. I learned that while you work out, your brain is releasing endorphins. This can release you from stress and create a feeling of well-being.

When you release endorphins, it triggers positive feelings. Endorphins can be released during pleasurable activities. Activities such as exercise, eating, and sex. They will reduce the receptor of pain and will instead spark your body into positivity.

So, I started to notice a pattern that developed over time. I was going to the gym depressed, and I was leaving the gym feeling amazing. It got to the point where the gym was doing more for me than the emotional therapy was. It was giving my mental health more benefit than my physical health.

When I would miss a day, I was a completely different person. I was pissy, aggravated, and easily annoyed with people. I started working out more for my mental health than my physical health. The physical process just became a perk to the effect exercise was having on my mental health. I would feel clear, open minded, and healthy after working out.

This was the biggest benefit I was getting from the gym. After about three months, I started going to the gym twice a day. And this went on for a good eight months. I was addicted to that high feeling.

Another benefit I was getting was, naturally, when your brain sees progress, it creates a mental high. When I noticed that last week, I was benching 155 and this week I'm benching 165, well, it felt amazing! I noticed that when I saw progress it was helping my emotions so much. And I became dependent on it.

So, I highly recommend everyone to exercise. You should take care of your body. I'm not saying you need to go and run a marathon. But just start doing *something*. Start off doing ten push-ups. Go outside and try to run a sprint. You're breathing and you're alive, and that's a blessing. *Do* something with your body. Start off simple and, I'm telling you, it gets better. You just have to take action.

My recommendation for people that struggle is to get into it. Go to the gym, or if a gym is not your scene, do some sort of physical activity for twenty-one straight days for only five minutes a day. Set an alarm, and when it hits five minutes, leave. If you do this for twenty-one days, it becomes a habit. Your brain now knows to wake up and go to the gym, or whatever time you go at. Once it becomes a routine, you're going to tell yourself you might as well be going to get something out of it. So, at this point you will begin working out.

Start thinking about exercise as a privilege instead of work. Be grateful every day you can wake up and move your body. Cause I'll tell you one thing for sure: there's a lot of people that wish they were in your position and could do that. Remember, "I get to," versus "I have to." The fact that you *get to* go the gym and move your body is a damn blessing. Believe me, I know from experience.

When I came out of the coma, I had lost a lot of weight from not moving a muscle for fourteen days. I did not eat, and I did not move. For fourteen full days. I weighed 130 pounds at six feet tall.

One year later, from working out and taking care of my body, and overcoming all the odds that were stacked against me, I weighed a lean 180 pounds. Growth.

CHINESE FARMER

"You never know what will be the consequence of the mis-
fortune; or, you never know what will be the consequences of
good fortune."
- Alan Watts

I'M GOING TO TELL YOU THE STORY ABOUT A
Chinese farmer who lives with his son. I discovered this
story from philosopher Alan Watts, and it benefited me in
many ways. Alan Watts is an English philosopher who is
known for popularizing Indian and Chinese traditions. This
is my interpretation of it.

The farmer lives with his son, and they have one horse.
One day, the horse runs away. Everyone from the town
comes by that night, the father tells them the horse ran
away, and the people respond, "Oh no, what terrible news."
The father looks at them and goes, "Maybe. I don't know if
it's good news or bad news yet. It's too soon to tell."

The next day, the farmer is working on his farm and the
horse comes running back. But this time, the horse comes
back with two horses beside him. Everybody from the town

comes over and goes, "Oh, wow! What great news! Your horse came back and now you have three!" The farmer responds, "Maybe. I don't know if it's good news or bad news. We don't know yet."

The next day, the son goes out to train one of the new horses. The horse rears back, and the son falls off and breaks his leg. Everybody from the town comes by and says, "Oh no! What terrible news." The farmer responds, "I don't know if it's good news or bad news. It's too soon to tell."

The next day, the military comes by the town and says they're taking all able-bodied young men to the military. The farmer looks at them and says, "My son has a broken leg, so he can't go to the military." Later that night, everyone from the town comes by and goes, "Oh, what good news! Your son didn't have to go to the military." The father says, "Good news or bad news, we don't know yet."

The point of the story is that people are always so quick to jump to conclusions on how good something is or how bad something is, but the truth is we don't always know right away how everything will pan out. It is so easy to just wish things were different, but further down the road it may end up working out in your best interest.

This story applies to my injury so well because I hated my life. I thought my injury was a curse and I thought it was the worst possible scenario imaginable when, the truth is, it ended up being the best thing that ever happened to me. Like I've said, I'll always hate the fear it instilled in my loved ones, but it completely changed the direction my life was going in. And I wouldn't change a thing.

I remember when I discovered this Alan Watts story, and I was still down on the way things were turning out for me. But I found it at the perfect time because I applied it to my life. I realized, as the farmer says, "Good or bad, who knows. It's too soon to tell," and began to apply that to my life.

VALUES

"Values are like fingerprints. Nobody's are the same,
but you leave 'em all over everything you do."
-Elvis Presley

EVA AND I WENT OUT TO DINNER ONE NIGHT, and everything was going smoothly. We both ordered cocktails, ordered cauli wings (if you've never tried them, highly recommend), and were really just enjoying each other's presence. Then I, being the deep thinker I am, decided to make things a bit more serious, per usual.

Eva finished laughing about what we were previously talking about when I decided to ask her, "What would you say are the three things you value most in your life? In order from first to third."

Eva stopped smiling, got serious, put her drink down, and started to think. "I don't know. I guess I would say my health at number one, my relationships at number two, and happiness at number three," Eva answered me.

"Those are great values, I'm honored I made it in there

at number two," I replied with a bit of a joking tone. "If you're going to ask mine, what are yours?" Eva replied.

"I don't really wanna share mine," I told Eva.

"Come on, you can't make me share mine and not share yours," Eva told me. I paused for a minute. "Are you sure you want me to tell you? You might not like mine," I said to Eva.

"Well now you're freaking me out, so you have to tell me," Eva said to me.

"Okay, okay, fine," I said to Eva. I put my drink down and looked at her. "But you have to let me at least explain my reasoning after, so you can't get mad right away." All the more I could tell her anxiety was increasing.

"Just tell me what they are," Eva said in frustration.

"Okay, okay," I told Eva.

"First and foremost is my health. Second is my purpose, and third is my relationships," I said.

I could tell it took her back a step, but like I said, I wanted to explain my reasoning. So, I continued on. "My health is first because I've learned it makes me a better person. When I get to the gym first thing in the morning, it makes me more present at work," I said. "When I feel good about what I'm putting in my body, it increases my moods. I find I'm just a better person. Therefore, it makes my other values like my purpose and my relationships more fulfilling," I continued.

"I understand that, but your purpose comes before me?" Eva said.

"This is the one that makes me emotional," I said to

Eva. "I agree. I understand how that could sound bad. But it's the truth. Because I know when the odds were nine-to-one that I wouldn't survive, that means I survived for a reason," I told Eva.

"I survived to share my story, to give people hope that even on the darkest of days, you have to remember the sun might come out tomorrow," I said. "I know it's not gonna be easy to get there, and it might seem like I'm crazy at first, but I have had these visions and I know God kept me alive to share my story and show my perspective on life after nearly losing it," I told Eva. "I can really feel it in my chest. This isn't for me, this is my purpose and I want to make a difference, even if it's the slightest bit."

She nodded her head. "Okay, I understand and respect that," Eva said to me.

"And third, my relationships," I told Eva. "I prioritize my family, you, and my friends so much. I really try to show the people I love how much I love them," I said with some emotion in my chest. "If there is one thing I learned from nearly never being able to speak again with the people I love, is that everything in life is temporary. Your job is temporary, your car is temporary, even your relationships can be temporary," I told Eva. "But while I have those relationships, I'm for damn sure gonna make sure they're good ones that make an impact," I said with a smile on my face.

Eva nodded her head and gave me a small grin.

Values are important in life. What you value is who you are, and it impacts you every day. For without even realizing it, your values become a part of your everyday decisions.

What you eat, who you hang out with, how you spend your free time, are all based around your values.

Make sure you prioritize your values, and make sure they're good ones.

WHAT IF?

"What if I fall? Oh, but my darling, what if you fly?"
-Erin Hanson

DURING MY RECOVERY, I HAD A LOT OF FREE time and no one to really hang out with besides my mom because all of my friends were away at college. So, I started to pick up hobbies. Like I said before, going to the gym was one, and so was reading. I also had a doctor tell me reading could help my working memory recover because I had to pay attention more and remember what was going on. So, I figured, why not give it a try.

The first book I read was *When Breath Becomes Air* by Paul Kalanithi. It is about a man battling cancer while working as a neurosurgeon. And although we had radically different stories, I felt some alignment to my life through it.

It's a very intriguing book. But I realized, since it was almost like I was starting all over again, I could use some self-help books. So, the second book I read was *You Can't Hurt Me* by David Goggins. If it weren't for this book, I wouldn't have had HALF the recovery I had. And I'll explain why.

You Can't Hurt Me is a crazy story about David Goggins's hard upbringing and how it made him who he is. David Goggins weighed in at 300 pounds while working for EcoLab, making $2,000 a month and living with his mom. He was, as he says and makes clear, a loser.

He then talks about how his life transformed, and he became a life-changing Navy SEAL motivational speaker and author. The book gets to a point where he talks about when people say, "What if?" A lot of people use "What if?" in a bad way. "What if I study for three hours, but fail the test?" "What if I ask the girl out and she says no?" It's natural for the brain to focus on the negative more than the positive, so people use "What if?" in a way that scares them from trying what they truly want to pursue. It's that fear of failure that keeps you from getting where you want to go.

Goggins turns around the way people use "What if?" Goggins uses "What if?" in a way that tells the mind to create the positive and imagine the outcome in the best way possible. "What if I go out for a run four days a week and I lose five pounds by the end of January?" "What if I study for my math test and get an A this time?" David Goggins uses "What if?" in a way to imagine what if the best scenario happens. So, I started to apply this.

In about March of 2020, I wrote on a Post-It note, "What if I have a recovery that didn't seem imaginable, went back to the College of Charleston, and got better grades than I did before my injury?" I carried around that Post-It note in my wallet with me every day, everywhere I went. Now, if you were someone who knew me at this time, you would read this Post-It note and think, "This guy is crazy." It didn't seem possible.

But I read this Post-It note multiple times a day. I created this vision in my head of this happening, and I worked my ass off for it to happen. Doing extra hours of therapy when I got home and really just taking care of my body and brain. Around May/June, it started to seem possible that I would make it back to Charleston.

And I did make it back to Charleston. I made it back to Charleston, and here were my first semester grades: B+, B, C+, C. My second semester grades: A-, B+, B, B, B. I know you can't see my transcript, but those are the best grades I have ever had in college. And they were after a traumatic brain injury. Ask yourself, "What if?"

Defy all odds.

If you want to change your life, change the quality of questions you ask yourself. Instead of having hardship happen in your life and saying out loud, "How could this happen to me?" maybe take a second to sit back and ask, "How can I use this to my advantage?"

If you sit there and wonder why something was so bad, your mind is just focusing on the negative in the situation. When you train your mind to do this, it is only going to attract more negativity to your life.

But if you have this hardship occur, and you sit back and wonder, "How can I use this to benefit me?" your mind will start to create scenarios with a positive outcome. If your mind begins to open up new possibilities, you can begin to take action.

BE A LION

*"A truly strong person does not need the approval of others,
any more thant a lion needs approval of sheep."*
-Vernon Howard

THERE'S A REASON WHY A LION IS ON THE front cover of this book. I discovered the importance of a lion's mentality from Eric Thomas. Eric Thomas is a well-known public speaker and author.

A lion is referred to as the King of the Jungle. But why is a lion the King of the Jungle? What made the lion the King of the Jungle? A lion isn't the biggest, an elephant is probably the biggest. Lions definitely aren't the fastest, a cheetah is the fastest animal in the jungle. A lion isn't the smartest. A chimpanzee is probably the smartest.

So, then what makes a lion the King of the Jungle?

His mindset. His mentality is what stands him apart from the rest of the animals in the jungle. Sometimes in life, it isn't about being the biggest or the strongest. It isn't always about being the smartest person in the room. But if you believe you are, and you work to be the best, you will separate yourself from the rest of the crowd. You would be an uncommon man amongst uncommon men.

This was a big change I had to make in my recovery. I created a lion mentality when approaching my day. I was attacking my day as hard as I could. Change your mentality from just being a part of the jungle. Don't just be a part of the crowd. Separate yourself. Know that you are the hardest working person in the group.

For me, I felt a big step in my growth process to separate myself from the rest was accomplishing something I really disliked. Working my way through something I didn't enjoy doing but finding a way to get it done. So, one night, I was watching TV at my apartment and I tried to think of what that thing to accomplish that I didn't like could be.

And the first thing that popped into my head was running. I've never been a big runner. I have found joy in strength training, but I have always found that running exhausts me. So, that was it. That night, I found out there was a half marathon in Charleston within a year and I signed up for it.

Once my credit card payment went through, this screen popped up on the website that said, "Once the payment goes through, there are no refunds." Oh boy, no turning around now.

But I needed that. Because since I signed up for something I did not like, I knew I couldn't turn around now, and I went into it one hundred percent. No half in, half out. I was all in.

When I go for a run, as I begin to feel fatigued, in my

head I can see myself leaving Kessler Institute in a wheel-chair. I can feel myself trying to jog in the Kessler parking lot as Amy cheers me on, legs so weak I needed her holding my shoulder.

I put myself in a state of vulnerability. And that is when the lion mindset kicks in. Remembering how low in life I was while I pushed myself beyond limits that were never possibly imaginable for me. A lion wouldn't throw himself to the wolves because he's feeling weak. A lion would find a way to build the mental strength to overcome the adversity that crosses his path.

So, that's what I did. And I still do. I try to build up mental fortitude to overcome what steps in my path.

IF YOU WANNA TAKE THE ISLAND, BURN YOUR BOATS

"Leaders who practice the law of victory believe that anything less than success is unacceptable. And they have no plan B."
-John Maxwell

IF YOU WANNA TAKE THE ISLAND, BURN YOUR boats. This is one of my favorite quotes and it was Tony Robbins who said it. Tony Robbins is an American author, public speaker, and self-improvement coach. Let me explain the meaning behind this quote. In life, there is always an escape route. There is always a reason to not do what you really need to do, or a boat to escape the island you intended to overtake. We create lifelines and exit routes when really all we need to do is burn the boats.

Say you want to take over an island. There might be another tribe on the island, but the island is really nice, and you want to take it over and make it home. So, you tie up your boat and make sure it's safe and sound. By leaving your boat docked up in the sand, in the back of your mind you always have that escape route. The boat is your plan B if plan A to overtake the island starts to get hard.

But here's the truth. People who have plan Bs are people who lose. If you want to take the island, you need to burn your boats. By burning your boat, well, now you have no choice. *You can't leave.* So, knowing you can't leave, you will do whatever the hell you need to do to take over that island.

A time when I first applied burning the boats was right when I was released from Kessler Institute and got the approval to live at home. And it was actually my mom who fueled the idea. Kessler sent me home with a wheelchair. They knew I was just learning how to get back on my feet, but it was probably safe to have a wheelchair, just in case.

Right when we got back to my house, I watched my mom wheel the wheelchair into the garage. "What are you doing? I'm going to need that to get from my room to the kitchen," I said to my mom.

"Not anymore you won't," my mom said back to me. "You're young and you've always been pretty athletic, you'll be able to walk from your room to the kitchen."

And right there, there was no longer a safe route. No more plan B. By putting away the wheelchair, I didn't have a choice anymore. No matter how uncomfortable, or how bad I wanted to feel for myself, I had to go through trial and error until I was comfortable on my two feet again.

Having a plan B is a safe option, but by burning your boats, it creates this fighter mentality that will not lose. The point is people quit too early and don't see things through.

Instead of taking the easy way out (the boat), focus on what you truly want to achieve.

FAIL FORWARD

*"Failure is simply the opportunity to begin again,
this time more intelligently."*
-Henry Ford

FROM THE SECOND WE'RE BORN WE ARE taught how bad it is to fail. If you fail a test, get cut from a basketball team, a girl dumps you, it's all bad. As a kid growing up, your parents may even punish you for it. If you fail a test your mom might say, "That's it, no more Xbox for the next month!" So, from the moment we're born, we train our minds that failure is something we should avoid.

When, in reality, failure should be the first step in going anywhere. Once you fail, now you know what not to do. If you are learning something new or doing something you've never done before, naturally you're going to fail. I learned that failure is a healthy part of the journey. Because failure is one of the best teachers in life. Sure, there are some people who are naturally gifted at certain things and it just comes easy for them. If that's the case, obviously you shouldn't intentionally fail.

But for most people in life, at some point, you are going to fail. And when you do, don't fail and give up. Don't fall short and tell yourself maybe it's not for you. Naturally, when you're not successful, your brain is going to say, "Well, looks like this isn't for me! I'm not doing this again!" No. Shift your mindset. Fail and fail forward.

Fail and then sit back and think about it. Think about what it is that you did wrong. Sometimes, it isn't even what we did wrong, but what we can do better. What it is that didn't work, and what you need to do differently to do better. Think about the different approaches you can take that can lead to success.

For me, as an athlete, I found that failure was just part of the journey. My jump shot would be struggling, so I changed the way I followed through. My hitting wasn't too good, so I adjusted my stance. You make a mistake, you learn from it, and you move forward.

Think about it, no baby ever walked the first time they tried. No, every child is going to stumble, take one more step, fall again, and then repeat. While this is going on, no parent looks at their child and says, "Yeah, sorry, maybe walking isn't for you." Of course not. They fall a thousand more times. The child fails walking and tries again. Fail and fail forward.

Failure became a necessary step towards achieving my goals. When I would fail to accomplish work in therapy, I would pause, realize how I could change what I was doing, and try again. Also, once you feel failure, well, now you know how much you dislike that feeling. And if you really dislike that feeling, you'll do what you can at all costs to grow from that feeling going forward.

I've learned to accept failure. Learn from failure. Grow from failure. 'Cause if there's one thing for damn sure, you aren't avoiding failure. It'll always be right around the corner depending on what your next step is. So, when you fail, don't give up. Don't run away. Accept it and get better.

Fail forward.

YOU VS. YOU

"The only person you should try to be better than
is the person you were yesterday."
-Anonymous

WE'RE ALL GUILTY OF COMPARING OURSELVES to other people. It's hard not to when it's so natural. If you're playing on a basketball team and someone is getting more time than you, but you think you should be playing more than him, you compare yourself to him. And you also try to single-handedly be better than he is. Now he has become your biggest competition.

Instead of trying to compete against someone else, it should always be you against you. You should try to be better than the person you were yesterday. And the reason for that is because only you know your advantages, disadvantages, your struggles, and everything in between.

Wake up in the morning and think to yourself, "Well, yesterday I shot well. I was playing good offense, but I need to work on my defense. My rebounding could be a little better." And then you go to practice and work your ass off at defense. When practice is over, you don't compare your defense to anyone else on the team. You compare your defense to yesterday's defense. When you notice improvement, then it's a job well done.

You vs. You was a big one during my recovery. I constantly found myself sitting home on my couch comparing myself to my friends. Comparing myself to my friends that were going to five college classes and partying on the weekends while I was going to therapy three days a week, couldn't drink alcohol, and was spending my Friday nights watching movies with my mom. Which, by doing this, only led to depressive thoughts, built up anger, and frustration.

When, the truth is, my friends didn't have a brain injury. My friends didn't lie in a coma for fourteen days. We really weren't comparable at all, yet I found myself constantly doing so.

I learned that no one has been on the same path as me, no one has been going through the same hardships as me, and therefore no one should be compared to me. I became my biggest competition. And I was pushing myself every day to be better than I was the day before. And it worked! You'll find when your focus zeroes in on less external forces and more so on what is in your control, you truly can improve who you are.

BREATHWORK

"The ability to breathe is a gift.
Wake up grateful each day for that gift."
-Brandt Reader

NO MATTER WHAT GENDER OR ETHNICITY, every person in the world has one thing in common, and that is breathwork. It's funny, though. Even though our body has to work all day every day to breathe, we really don't think about it very much. But what if I told you every feeling and every emotion all changes with your breath?

I've noticed that when I'm calm, I breathe slowly and very peacefully. I notice when I'm anxious, I'll be tapping my foot and breathing a little faster.

It is important to notice how it changes because you have full control over your breathing. If you stop and take a minute, you can completely change your breathwork. It is important to know how to control your breathwork because you can change your mood. Something I like to do to change my breathwork I learned from Jay Shetty. It's called box breathing. Box breathing is a highly trained Navy SEAL technique. Navy SEALs use box breathing before entering highly pressured situations. It is when you breathe in for four seconds, hold for four seconds, breathe out for four seconds, and hold for four seconds. Just like a box.

I usually do this for about three to four minutes. Box breathing is a very good way to stop your mind from becoming anxious. When I start feeling anxiety come upon my body, or I notice my mind is racing, I do box breathing for about four minutes. This is like a restart for me. It calms my mind and brings me back to where I want it to be. Box breathing is a very healthy way to calm yourself down when you start to get worked up.

By learning how to take leverage of my breathing, I learned how to control my emotions, how to maintain mental calmness, and therefore tackle the challenges life throws at me in a healthier manner. As I stated earlier, by changing your breathing, you can change your moods. If you learn how to change your breathwork, you will notice your life change for the better.

CHANGE

"Change the way you look at things
and the things you look at change."
-Wayne Dyer

WHEN YOU'RE IN HIGH SCHOOL AND YOU graduate, often someone will write in your yearbook, "Good luck and don't change!" When really, *life is always changing*. Throughout your whole life you're constantly changing and playing different characters of yourself.

The character you were when you were five years old playing tee ball is different from the character you were when you asked out your first girlfriend. And the character you were when you asked out your first girlfriend is different from the character you were when you were getting ready to send your kids to college. Your whole life you will be constantly evolving into a new version of yourself.

More people need to be welcoming of change. If not welcoming, then at least be accepting of change. Being open to change invites growth. Growth brings some growing pains, but when you experience these growing pains, you also expand who you are. And the expansions you are making are what changes you and the world around you.

Change can feel like one of the scariest things in the world. No one really likes to change. Change can feel like an uncomfortable period of your life where you don't really know who you are, where you are, or what's coming next. It isn't easy, but you need to learn how to flow with change. You need to accept that the character you are is disintegrating, and a new chapter of your life is unfolding.

Some chapters are exciting, some are scary, and some are sad. But the important thing to know is that they are all necessary. They are all necessary, and they are all temporary. They all contain lessons that help to shape you into the best version of who you are meant to be.

Think about who you were five years ago. What about yourself today would the version of you five years ago be happy to see has changed? What about yourself today would the version of you five years ago be upset to see has changed? Take some time to sit back and acknowledge this. First off, be proud of yourself for the growth you've made in the right direction. Next, from here, make some changes to benefit you going forward.

When I think back to me five years ago, and I reflect on the pieces I took with me and the pieces I dropped, it really puts things in perspective. When you're living life day by day, you don't notice the incremental changes. But over time, those incremental changes build up. And they compound into either a positive outcome or a negative outcome.

I think if the version of me five years ago could see

how I have changed, I would be pretty content. Content with the positive lifestyle habits I have added to my life and the lessons I have learned from the hard times. I think the version of me five years ago would maybe even laugh at the thought of me possibly changing this much. Change is scary. But it's also necessary. I'm grateful for every step along the way.

GO ONE MORE

"When you're stuck between a challenge and giving up,
take one more step.
That one step can totally change your life."
-Ilchi Lee

WHETHER IT'S WORK, BEING AT THE GYM, OR spending time with family, we all reach that point where our brains are ready to call it quits. We all reach that point where we say to ourselves, "That's it. I've had enough, I think I'm done now," and we call it quits. That inner voice in your head thinks you have reached your max and it is ready to tap out. But what if I told you to just hang in there a little longer? What if I told you doing one more can make the biggest difference in your life?

When your mind feels like it has reached its potential, but you do one more of whatever you are doing, you are telling yourself that you are stronger than your mind. You are telling that inner voice in your head that you are the boss. I don't believe you were placed on this earth to barely get by. You truly were born to do something great. And the first step in getting there is to do one more.

If you're at the gym and you feel you're starting to get tired on the treadmill, run for just one more minute. If you're a salesman and the clock is at 4:58 and you're off at 5, make just one more sales call. If you know your mom is going through a hard time, give her one more call and make sure she's okay. These ideas I'm throwing out there seem so miniscule, but I'm telling you that applying this "one more" mindset can absolutely transform your life.

You will open doors in your life that you didn't know existed. By doing one more, you will build more confidence, more discipline, and really just mental strength because you're noticing you are capable of more than you thought. You are 100% capable of creating the life you dream of.

And, the truth is, it all begins with doing one more. The more you begin to act upon these subtle changes, the more your life will begin to change.

My recommendation: grab a pen and paper and write down a goal. And I recommend it to be a goal that is pretty far for you to reach. Next, write down step by step how to reach that goal. Even if you don't know how to, write down what you think would help to reach that goal. And now begin to act upon it. Start with step one and keep working up until that goal becomes a reality.

TIME

"Life is a race against disappearing time."
-Sunday Adelaja

I HAD A TRAUMATIC EXPERIENCE THAT MADE me realize everyone's time on this earth is limited. Your time on this earth isn't forever. There are sixty seconds in a minute. Sixty minutes in an hour. And twenty-four hours a day. You can't add more time to your life. No matter what you tell yourself. There is no changing that simple fact.

Although we don't usually view it from this perspective, it is important to realize that time is an asset. And time is the most important asset that you have. When your time is up, you get no chance to go back and do things differently. Once it's said and done, that's a wrap.

So, it's simple. Try to make the most of every second you have on this earth. You can say, "Oh, I'll get around to that in an hour." You can say, "Oh, right, I'll get around to that tomorrow." But the truth is, there is going to come a day where you don't have a tomorrow.

So, tell the people you love that you love them. Take

a drive to the beach and go see that sunset one more time. Everyone has a different purpose in their life, but use your time to do what you love and don't look back wishing you could change a single thing.

I live my life having no regrets because I know that's just a waste of my energy. No matter how much I regret something, it for damn sure won't change that it happened. I went through a short period of time regretting that I ever hopped on that skateboard. I would tell myself that if I never jumped on that skateboard, I never would have nearly died. I would tell myself how different my life would be if I didn't have a traumatic brain injury.

But after a few months, I realized that no matter how long I spent thinking about the different circumstances, my life wasn't getting any better. It actually felt like I was regressing. No matter how much you write the script differently in your head, it won't change the reality of how you use your time. Prioritize your time. Make the most of who you are and where you apply yourself.

EQUANIMITY

"Equanimity is a perfect unshakab.le balance of mind."
-Nyanponika Thera

EQUANIMITY IS SOMETHING I LEARNED FROM
Ed Mylett. For a simpler understanding, equanimity is being peaceful and having mental calmness in a world full of
craziness. Equanimity is a philosophy that goes back to the
beginning of time.

I discovered Sir William Osler's most famous 1889 es-
say defining equanimity. Equanimity is trying to find seren-
ity while you are battling the challenges life throws at you.
You're going to get shit thrown at you in life. You can try as
hard as you want, but there is no avoiding that. While you
can't control life's external forces, you can control how you
think and how you react to them.

It is important to try and quiet your mind when life
gets difficult. And that is essentially what equanimity is.
Equanimity is when you have a stressful day at work, your
boss just won't stop blaming you for his problems, you get
in the car to drive home, and your tire is flat. Then you

finally get home and your roommates are all hanging out in the living room.

You don't start yelling at your roommates to chill out and be quiet. You remind yourself of equanimity. Your roommates aren't the reason your boss was making your life difficult. Your roommates aren't the reason your tire was flat. So, therefore, you shouldn't take it out on them just because they're having fun.

You take a deep breath, you calm down for a second, and you greet them respectfully. It is important to remember that every feeling in life is temporary. No matter what is happening in your life right now, it will not last forever.

Meditation has helped me a lot with equanimity. For me, when I can take fifteen minutes to just be alone with my own thoughts, remind myself of the importance of mental calmness and not letting external influences get in the way, I handle my responsibilities much better. Equanimity is something we have to practice every day. For life will continue to throw challenges, and we will continue to work on staying calm.

DELAYED GRATIFICATION

*"The ability to discipline yourself to delay gratification
in the short term in order to enjoy greater rewards in the long
term, is the indispensable prerequisite for success."*
-Brian Tracy

WE LIVE IN A SOCIETY WHERE WE AREN'T RE-
ally taught about delayed gratification. We live in a world
where we want instant gratification and don't want to do
the work that takes time.

When I began my fitness journey, I went to the gym
one day, came home, looked in the mirror, and I noticed
nothing. So, I went to the gym again the next day, came
home and looked in the mirror, and I noticed nothing. If
I'm going to the gym and I'm not noticing anything, what's
the point of even going, right?

However, around day thirty of going to the gym, I
looked in the mirror and noticed progress. I noticed the
person looking back was not the same person from day one.

This is delayed gratification. Sometimes in life you ar-
en't going to get what you want on the first try. Sometimes

it will take repetition and hard work to notice progress. But when you hit that first milestone, you will look back and realize how good it feels to have made that progress.

Habits need to be persistent in order to see change. Habits take time and effort, they don't happen overnight. Then, you will begin to see change. And when you see that change, a feeling of joy will overcome your body. You will feel pride in yourself that even though you were doing work and not getting immediate reward, you stayed disciplined enough to continue working.

Delayed gratification teaches you patience and will give you lots of faith in trusting the journey you are on. Delayed gratification can be applied to many more places than just going to the gym. For example, eating healthy to try and lose weight. You're not going to eat one meal and shed ten pounds. But over time, by eating healthy, maintaining discipline in the long-term goal you want and not the short-term pleasure, you can accomplish the goal you have in mind.

When you become more aware of delayed gratification, you will become more mindful of the practice. For it certainly is not easy. However, when you feel the reward of it, you will build up the composer to work your way through it.

GOALS

"If you want to be happy, set a goal that commands your thoughts, liberates your energy and inspires your hopes."
-Andrew Carnegie

I WILL ALWAYS SAY THAT PEOPLE SHOULD SET goals because goals give you a sense of direction. However, goals aren't what get you where you want to go. Goals are good because while you are on the journey of accomplishing a goal, you should be making progress along the way. And even if you don't accomplish the goal, you'll definitely end up closer than before you started.

What's more important than goals are micro habits. Micro habits are the little actions you take on a consistent basis. Truth is, goals can be very generalized. By a generalized goal, I mean there can be many people that have the same idea in mind. And, therefore, people can have the same goal in common. And when everyone has a goal to win the championship, well, only one team can do that.

Yet the micro habits, like what you do at practice every day, how you're spending your days off, who you're choosing to surround yourself with, these micro habits can make a huge difference. Because what you're doing at practice every day will affect what you do in a game. How you're spending your days off will affect what you do on the days you don't have off. Who you're choosing to surround yourself with affects who you will become.

So, in the moment, these micro habits seem so tiny, but what you don't notice is what these micro habits can become. These micro habits will have a snowball effect. And as they're rolling down the hill, the snowball (the micro habits) will get bigger and bigger. And before you know it, they build up to the big goal that you originally set for yourself.

In order to achieve your goals, start by setting micro habits. For these micro habits will expand and lead you to goals that you dream of fulfilling.

THE ANGEL
AND THE DEVIL

"If I got rid of my demons, I'd lose my angels."
-Tennessee Williams

THROUGH MY SPIRITUAL JOURNEY, I HAVE
been able to take a step back when life throws me situations.
Whether they're good or bad, I'm able to look at them from
a different perspective. Our whole lives growing up we've
seen the picture of the person when an altercation occurs,
and they have the devil on one shoulder and the angel on
the other. Typically, the devil is whispering the more fun,
but dangerous route while the angel is whispering the safer,
but more righteous route.

I've discovered this is an extremely accurate analogy of
life. For example, you'll be out with your friends, and you'll
have four or five beers, and your friend asks you to drive
home. You know you're not drunk, but you know it might
not be the best idea to get behind the wheel since you con-
sumed more than the legal limit.

You know it's not a far drive, but you know it might be

smarter to just do the walk even though it'll take an extra fifteen minutes. Your friend is telling you to just drive because it's a little rainy, it'll save time, and you'll be fine. The angel in your head is telling you to just walk, play it safe, and pick up the car tomorrow.

Your friend in this situation is like the devil in your ear telling you to get behind the wheel while the voice in your head is like the angel telling you to just play it safe and walk.

Now by no means am I calling any of your friends the devil, I am just saying, in this situation, this is when life throws tests at you. I've realized life rewards you when you choose the higher road and life punishes you when taking the darker road.

Say you said to yourself, "I'll be okay to drive home," and got behind the wheel. Next thing you know, you're about a block away from home so you look down to turn the music off and you hit a parked car. This is life when taking the path that the devil was telling you to take.

Now, say you decided to walk instead of drive. You get out of your friend's house and begin walking. You realize it's colder out than you thought and start thinking to yourself, "Damn, maybe I made the wrong choice," when all of a sudden you hear a car horn and it's one of your buddies. "Hop in the car, man, it's freezing!!" and he drives you home. This is like the angel on your shoulder rewarding you for taking the higher road.

Now, I just made this scenario up, and I'm not saying life will reward you every time you take the higher road. But I have realized that when you make the more responsible decision, life tends to work in your favor. Try to be the best version of yourself that you can be and watch when life rewards you.

My mentor, Paul Melella, taught me about the different voices we have in our heads. Paul helped me to identify the voices in my head and recognize when they start to speak up. We did this by naming each voice and giving character traits to notice when they start to be the voice in my head.

Everyone typically has a few voices in their heads. My main few are Doubting Dylan, Dominate Dylan, and Defeated Dylan.

Doubting Dylan is that voice in my head that always assumes the worst outcome will occur. It is the voice in my head that sees the path I want to take in life but begins to think of every reason why I shouldn't take that path.

Dominate Dylan is the voice in my head that praises who I am and where I am going in life. Dominate Dylan is the voice when I'm at the gym and, when I start to feel a little fatigued, wakes me up and says, "You're not this weak, you've been through a lot more hardships than this," and does one more set at the gym. Dominate Dylan will overcome any situation thrown on my path no matter how big or small.

Defeated Dylan is the voice in my head that is thrown in a battle and wants to wave the white flag. Defeated Dylan thinks it's been a long day and it's time to call it quits.

It's important to get a pen and paper and write down when you begin to hear these different versions of you speak up. It's important because, through repetition, I have learned to identify when I sense that version of me speaking up. And when I do, I either redirect my thoughts or I power through whatever is going on. Everyone has different voices in their head. Take some time to get to know yours and work with them.

CHOOSE YOUR HARD

"Life is hard. After all, it kills you."
-Katherine Hepburn

IF THERE IS ONE THING I'VE LEARNED FOR sure, is that life is hard. Whether it's financially, physically, mentally, or emotionally, life is going to get hard. But the truth is, you can get to choose your hard. And let me explain how.

Working out is hard. You're waking up an hour earlier, driving to the gym, and putting your body in physical exhaustion. But looking in the mirror and feeling lack of confidence and not liking what is looking back is hard, too. Do you want to look in the mirror and not be content or do you want to add more work to your schedule? Choose your hard.

Relationships are hard. Living with someone day in and day out, balancing work, your partner, your hobbies, etc. is hard. You think one thing is right, but your partner thinks the opposite is right, so it leads to a fight. But break ups are hard, too. You shared a lot of your precious time with someone, made changes to your life to suit the relationship that didn't last. Choose your hard.

Looking for a job that fits your purpose is hard. It means turning down potential offers that you may not love, maybe taking less money than a job you said no to, and looking for a job all over again. But working a job you hate is hard, too. It means day in and day out you're doing the same thing over and over again. It means going to the same place with the same people that leads to unhappiness every day. So, now you get to choose your hard.

The truth is life will never be easy. It will always be hard. But you get to choose which hard you want. I've learned it's important to choose the hard things that will benefit you in the future and not the hard things that will give you temporary pleasure. Don't choose the things that are easy now but will make your future hard. Choose your hard wisely.

MEDITATION

"Meditation is like a gym in which you develop the powerful mental muscles of calm and insight."
-Ajahn Brahm

I WAS TAKING ADVICE FROM ANYONE ON WAYS to help me with my depression and controlling my emotions. And one common answer to my issues was meditation. I always viewed meditation as something the crazy people did or something that was weird. However, I realized I was consistently hearing about the health benefits and how good meditation is for your mind. So, I began to give it a try.

I will start off by saying one thing: meditation is FAR from easy. It took me months of practice until I really started to get something from it. If there is one thing for certain, mediation takes discipline. You need to be patient, and you need to be calm.

I saw this quote about meditation, and it was the perfect way to describe it. It said,

'So, what do you gain from meditation?' And the man

said, 'Nothing. But let me tell you what I've lost: anger, depression, anxiety, insecurity, fear of old age, and fear of death.'

And I think that this is the best way to describe meditation. It isn't that you gain a whole lot, but you release a lot that you should not keep bottled in. It will make you feel more pure. It will make you feel a load come off your back and help you realize you are okay right where you are.

I learned how to meditate from reading *Think Like a Monk* by Jay Shetty. Jay Shetty really breaks it down step by step and the different ways to meditate. The most important thing is being able to fully clear your mind. In your mind, hold nothingness. Picture blackness and really try to be as still as you can.

The three different types of mediation I do the most are breathwork, visualization, and mantras. You can do them individually; I like to do them for five to seven minutes each. What I do is set a timer for five minutes and focus on my breathing. When the timer goes off, I click repeat and move on to visualization. I do this for another five minutes, and when the timer goes off, I do another five minutes of mantras.

Breathwork is when you solely focus on just breathing. How you feel when you breathe in, and how you feel when you breathe out. Focus on how you feel from your toes all the way up your body, and all the way up to your head. To how you feel when you breathe out. And when you breathe in, you're breathing in love, confidence, faith, or really whatever you feel you need more of in your life. And when you breathe out, you are breathing out fear, anxiety, nervousness, or whatever you want to get rid of in your life. This will help you release the emotions you don't want and focus on the emotions you do.

I also like to do box breathing when I am doing breathwork. I usually try to do breathwork for around seven minutes.

Next, I do visualization. I visualize where I am now, and where I want to be. Then, I try to visualize the steps it takes to get there. It is important to see and feel yourself where you want to be, but it is more important to visualize yourself doing the steps it takes to get there. And really feel it. Feel how good it feels as you take one step closer to where you want to be. Imagine that successful feeling of getting what you want in life.

For example, I would visualize myself walking across the stage at graduation before I even came back to Charleston. In my head I would picture the crowd, feel the white tuxedo on my body, feel the sun rays on my skin, and hear the crowd clapping as my name was being announced. And then I would play back the steps it took to get there like being in class, doing homework, etc.

And lastly, I say mantras for a good five to seven minutes. And I say them in the present tense. I say something like, "I am grateful I am finishing this semester with As and Bs." Or something like, "I am grateful my working memory is improving everyday." The more you do this, over and over again, the more your subconscious mind will believe it. Remember, your subconscious doesn't know the difference between the truth and a lie, so speak into existence what you want to happen. And really believe that it is true. There is a good app called "ThinkUp" where you can record yourself saying mantras and make different categories for certain mantras.

I have grown so much from meditation that I still find myself starting my day off with it. I highly recommend you to challenge yourself. See how it makes you feel. Do it for one week and notice if it changes your moods, your habits, or your reactions to what life throws at you. Start just doing it for five to ten minutes and see if it helps you. See if you can find some mental clarity and learn to find joy in it.

RAS

"It all begins and ends in your mind. What you give power to, has power over you, if you allow it."
-Leon Brown

EVER TELL YOUR MOM SOMETHING LIKE, "I haven't seen Liam in so long," then you get in your car to go to get some food and it just so happens that you drive past Liam? Have you ever been talking with your friend and you're like, "Ferraris are cool but a Tesla X is definitely my favorite car," and then an hour or two later you're driving to your friend's house and you drive past a Tesla X?

What if I told you this wasn't a coincidence? What if I told you there was a science behind all of this happening? And the secret formula to this happening is called your RAS. Your Reticular Active System. Your RAS is like a filter in your brain. That Tesla X you just saw on the road didn't just happen to be there. That Tesla X was always there. It's just that now you're seeing it because it became a part of your RAS. Tesla Xs have now been filtered into your conscious mind since they have become so important to you.

This carries over to other parts of your life more than just seeing cars on the road. You buy a new pair of Converse sneakers and now it's like everywhere you go you see Converse sneakers. They were always there, they just weren't something you were visualizing or thinking about. Through repeated visualizations and thoughts, you can teach your mind what to focus on and move towards.

When you repeat your thoughts and your visualizations, you are telling your RAS what to pay attention to.

So, here is the crazy reality. If you feed your RAS positive thoughts and positive visualizations, you can truly attract what you want into your life. Sometimes you just need to slow down, filter out the thoughts you don't want, and focus on what you want to attract. Repetition will create opportunities in your life that you can't even imagine were possible.

GROWTH

"Change your perspective, and you change your reality."
- Dylan Finn

AS I WRAP UP MY STORY, I FEEL THIS IS AN IM-portant moment. As I shared all the amazing lessons I have learned along the way, I also shared quotes that impact-ed me during that time period of my life. So, as I sit here writing this last section, I thought to myself, how powerful would it be if I ended it with a quote written by myself?

If you change your perspective, you change your whole reality. This is a mantra that I made up months after I al-ready had an amazing recovery. Because I realized, once I changed the way I interpreted what happened to me, it completely changed the way I approached life. It changed the emotions I felt, the decisions I made, and, really, who I wanted to come out of this injury as. Truth is, if I ap-proached my recovery differently, and I had a "woe is me" mentality, I probably wouldn't have had the recovery I had. If I sat there and felt bad for myself, making every excuse

I could for why I shouldn't have to work hard, I wouldn't have this outlook on life I do now.

But once I changed my perspective, my whole entire reality changed. And yours can, too.

———

I titled my book *GROWTH*, and I saved this one for last for a reason. Growth is the biggest message behind my story. And truthfully, growth is one of the biggest elements in life. You are always going to be either growing or regressing. It's pretty difficult to hit a standstill in life and not go in one direction or the other.

Life is growth. And when mine seemed like it was really going to be moving in the wrong direction, I turned it around and learned how to use it to my advantage. I found a way to change my perspective and, therefore, change my future.

I'm just going to say it point blank: life isn't easy. Mine isn't and yours isn't, either. So, if we know this, if we know that life is going to be hard, why not try to put a smile on your face and make the most of it? Cause I'll tell you one thing for sure, complaining and crying about it won't make it any easier.

Whether you are where you want to be in life, or you have no idea how to get there, always strive for growth. Even when things look picture perfect, I promise you there is something you can continue to improve upon. And when you do, when you feel that improvement, that's what makes life so special. Knowing that the person you are today is a better version than the person you were yesterday.

The key to growth is to never stop believing. Don't let that negative voice in your head control you. Know you are destined for greatness, know you can overcome obstacles, and know that you can keep moving forward. If the strength you have can get you this far, that means it can take you even further than you can ever imagine.

I am currently writing this looking out my backyard window as the sun beams down on the stream. I'm listening to meditation music and as I sit here, I reflect on that twenty-one-year-old kid with a brain injury who couldn't multiply six-times-seven and wanted to end it all. And as I watch the water flow down this stream, and I look back on that version of me, I'm beyond grateful that I didn't.

For every hard time taught me a lesson, and those lessons formed me into a better version of myself. And for all the blessings, well, that's just what makes life so beautiful. There is nowhere else I'd rather be, no one else I'd rather be with, and I wouldn't want to have gone through anything easier than this journey I've been on.

Life is Growth. Wake up tomorrow and work a little harder than you did today. Take some time to appreciate everything you have and every good and bad moment you've ever been through in your life. For your life is a movie.

You're the main character and you're writing the script. Let's make it a good one.

AUTHOR'S NOTE

In this book, I have shared many lessons from inspirational leaders, public speakers, and authors that have helped me to transform my life. I have done my very best to acknowledge each and every one of them for their quotes and lessons that have helped me grow. Out of the lessons I have attributed to this book, I hope you can take away at least one lesson that may help you grow into a better version of yourself.

ABOUT THE AUTHOR

Dylan Finn was born and raised in Sea Girt, NJ.
He currently lives in Charleston,SC.
GROWTH is Dylan's first book and he is excited to share
his story with the world.
Please visit www.dylan-finn.com to learn more.

www.ingramcontent.com/pod-product-compliance
Lightning Source LLC
Chambersburg PA
CBHW071740120626
46550CB00002B/602